COMHAIRLE CHONTAE ROSCOMÁIN
LEABHARLANN CHONTAE ROSCOMÁIN

Home-Grown Vegetables

Diana Galligan

Home-Grown Vegetables

*Inspiration and practical advice
for would-be smallholders*

First published in the United Kingdom in 2007 by
Collins & Brown
10 Southcombe Street
London W14 0RA

An imprint of Anova Books Company Ltd

Published in association with The National Trust
(www.nationaltrust.org.uk) and The National Magazine Company
Limited. Country Living (www.countryliving.co.uk) is a trademark of
The National Magazine Company.

Commissioning Editor: Miriam Hyslop
Design Manager: Gemma Wilson
Illustrator: Carmen Carreira-Villar
Designer: Bill Mason
Editor: Jennie Buist Brown
Senior Production Controller: Morna McPherson

ISBN 978-1-84340-417-0

A CIP catalogue for this book is available from the British Library.

10 9 8 7 6 5 4 3 2 1

Reproduction by Spectrum Colour Ltd, UK
Printed and bound by MPG Books Ltd, Cornwall

This book can be ordered direct from the publisher.
Contact the marketing department, but try your bookshop first.
www.anovabooks.com

HOME-GROWN VEGETABLES

FOREWORD

Welcome to *Home-Grown Vegetables* which, along with *Home-Grown Fruit*, *Beekeeping* and *Henkeeping*, is one of the books that make up this new *Country Living* and National Trust series on becoming more self-sufficient. Nowadays, we are all very concerned about where our food comes from, how it has been produced, how far it has travelled to reach the supermarket shelves and, most importantly perhaps, how the environment may have been damaged in the process. The National Trust helps and encourages farmers to reach and maintain the highest environmental and animal welfare standards, and both the National Trust and *Country Living* champion local, organic food and sustainable practices by British growers. Now, with help from these excellent guides you, too, can begin to produce enough organic and tasty food in your own garden or allotment – honey, fruit, vegetables and eggs – to help feed you and your family throughout the year.

There is nothing quite like being able to pop out to the garden to pick fresh, tender vegetables for dinner knowing that, when you grow your own, the only 'food miles' travelled will be those between your plot and your kitchen. In recent years, there has been a surge of interest in 'growing your own' with the demand for allotments now at an all time high. Working outside on your own patch of land, having control over what you and your family consume, brings a huge feeling of satisfaction. Cooperating with nature as you grow tomatoes for the summer or parsnips for the winter months, being in touch with your environment and, of course, getting your hands dirty, is therapeutic in every way. Full of practical information and charming illustrations, this excellent guide by Diana Galligan will inspire you to join the ranks of people up and down the UK who are reaping the benefits of growing their own vegetables.

Susy Smith
Editor, *Country Living*

John Stachiewicz
Publisher, The National Trust

WHY GROW VEGETABLES?

Fresh, tender, succulent vegetables, on your plate within hours – if not minutes – of them being picked from the ground or from the stalk. What better incentive is there for growing your own veg?

THIRTY YEARS AGO organically grown vegetables were only available in specialised stores or small, local outlets. Today they occupy shelves in all the major supermarkets. But there is no getting away from the fact that many vegetables have been kept in a cold store, irradiated, washed in chlorine to destroy bacteria and treated with preservatives to prolong shelf life. They have been transported miles up and down the country and across seas and continents before they even get within sight of a plate. All this at a cost to the environment, the loss of vitamins and minerals, and potential long-term effects on our health.

When you grow your own, there are no 'food miles' involved. The only preservatives needed to store them, the natural ones of earth, damp sand, air and a cool, frost-free environment. You will know that it is the humus-rich soil, chemical-free feed, water and care and attention that you have given them that have produced the flavoursome vegetables you are about to eat.

Growing your own means you can eat good wholesome food as it comes into season, and by staggering sowings you can extend that season so not everything comes ready at the same time. With careful planning, you can feed yourself and your family with homegrown vegetables for the whole year. And share any excess with friends and neighbours.

Growing vegetables is not an exact science – and the effects of climate change are beginning to turn established dos and don'ts on their head. There are few right or wrong answers, only general advice. It may take a few years, but get to know your soil, its benefits and drawbacks, learn the rhythms of the seasons and the vagaries of the weather in your own particular area, then work with that, no matter what the book says. When it comes to your land, you're the expert. It's primarily a question of commonsense as well as confidence – and that comes with experience.

Growing vegetables should also be fun. Experiment with some of the more exotic types that are starting to appear in seed catalogues. Try some of the heritage varieties, or grow familiar vegetables in unfamiliar colours – purple carrots for instance, black sweetcorn, or white aubergines. Aim for the smallest, sweetest peas, or the largest, plumpest marrow. Whatever you do, enjoy!

YOUR VEG PLOT

Take time to get to know your plot. The best will have an open aspect that gets the sun for most of the day. Trees or high hedges will provide shelter from winds, but dense shade or dropping leaves will impede growth. Avoid slopes if possible as they are subject to soil erosion and are harder to work, but if it can't be avoided, work across the slope rather than down it, although you might need to consider building terraces if the slope is very steep. Equally, low ground is often a frost pocket and can become badly waterlogged – improving the soil with organic matter or p roviding a soakaway may help. You will need a convenient water source. And space for a shed or somewhere to store your tools and sundries so you don't have to carry everything back and forth. If there is room for a greenhouse on the site, that's a bonus, but it can always be positioned elsewhere. You also need to allocate a spot for a compost bin.

THE SOIL

To find out what type of soil you have, try the rain test. Pick up a handful after it has rained: if it feels gritty, it's sandy; if it's silky, it's silt; and if it feels sticky, then it's clay. Both silt

Thinning out seedlings/young plants

and clay will form a ball when moulded. Loam – the ideal –
is a mixture of all three. Thin, pale soils are low in humus
and often infertile. Heavy soils, which are dark, crumbly and
'peaty', are slow to drain and easily waterlogged. Dig over
heavy soils in the autumn so frosts can break them down
before the spring and work in sharp sand, grit and organic
matter to improve drainage. Add well-rotted compost or
organic matter to light soils, cover through the winter and
dig in spring for best results.

A simple pH test (available from garden centres) will show
whether the soil is neutral, acid or alkaline. A pH of 7 is
neutral, above 7 is alkaline, below 7 is acid. Add lime to
counteract the acid; add manure and compost if it's too
alkaline.

BEDS

A series of raised, narrow beds, approximately 90–150cm
(3–5ft) wide have the advantage over fewer, wider rectangular
beds. They are easier to manage and work, saving time and
backache. Yields are greater as spacing between plants doesn't
have to allow for access. They maintain high levels of organic
material and fertility – good for organic gardeners – and
working from paths either side means you can reach the
middle without walking on the soil, which avoids compaction

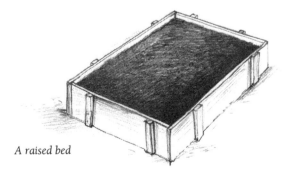

A raised bed

so you won't have to dig them over so regularly. Don't make them any longer than 3m (10ft) or you'll be tempted to cut across them rather than walk round, and plant in short rows side to side or in squares.

PATHS

Keep to a minimum of 30–38cm (12–15in) wide, but consider having the main ones wide enough to get a wheelbarrow down. Paths should be low maintenance; brick or paving slabs are ideal, but you could lay a weed-suppressant membrane after clearing the area and cover it with gravel or bark. Old carpet is another idea, but it will eventually rot down and need replacing, and while grass can look attractive, it will need frequent mowing.

Dry bark walkway

CROP ROTATION

This is the practice of grouping together closely related vegetables – legumes, brassicas and root crops – and moving them on year by year to a different bed to cut down on pests and diseases and minimise the loss of nutrients from the soil. Generally, it follows a four-year cycle, but you can extend the cycle by giving certain crops a bed of their own, such as onions, potatoes (which are a ground-clearing crop so useful

12

for improving the soil) or green manure crops (see page 20). The onion family, pumpkin family, leaves and salads, stem and fruiting vegetables can be fitted in where there is space. Perennials will need a bed of their own. A typical three-bed plan could work like this:

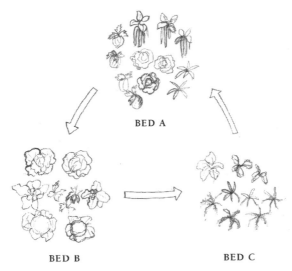

BED A

BED B   BED C

Crop rotation over four years

YEAR 1

BED A   LEGUMES PLUS ONION FAMILY
   Dig in plenty of manure or compost. Leave the nitrogen-rich roots in the soil to rot down for the brassicas.

BED B   BRASSICAS PLUS SALADS
   Dig in leafmould or compost and lime the soil if it's acid to protect against clubroot. Mulch in autumn ready for root crops.

BED C   ROOT CROPS PLUS STEM AND FRUITING VEGETABLES
   Dig in plenty of compost. You could sow green manure ready for the legumes next year.

YEAR 2
BED A Brassicas plus salads
BED B Root crops plus stem and fruiting vegetables
BED C Legumes plus onion family

YEAR 3
BED A Root crops plus stem and fruiting vegetables
BED B Legumes plus onion family
BED C Brassicas plus salads

YEAR 4
BED A Legumes plus onion family
BED B Brassicas plus salads
BED C Root crops plus stem and fruiting vegetables

COMPOST BIN

When planning the layout of your vegetable plot, it's very important to allow space for a compost bin or, ideally, bins. It takes three to six months to achieve good compost, so if you have three, side by side, you will have one to use, one that is rotting down, and one you can add to. You can buy bins in a variety of materials, but building one yourself is relatively easy and inexpensive and can be modelled to fit the space. You can use three pallets nailed together, with a fourth fixed so it's easily removable to act as a "door". Fill the gaps with straw, cardboard or newspaper and make a lid from old carpet or board. Or fix wire mesh to four corner stakes, line with cardboard and make a lid for it as before. To rot down, the contents need warmth, bacterial activity and moisture. Leave the bottom open to allow the worms access and add a good mixture – about half and half – of 'green' and 'brown' materials in layers. Mix it all together at intervals and water if it looks too dry.

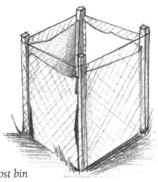

Wooden frame compost bin

'Green' materials include weeds, vegetable trimmings, lawn clippings and soft prunings; 'brown' materials include paper, tree leaves, straw and eggshells. Think of composting as making a fruit salad and chop up the materials to manageable sizes before adding them. If it's slow to get started add an activator. You can buy one readymade from garden centres, but farm manure, rabbit and poultry droppings, human urine, nettles, seaweed and comfrey leaves work just as well. As a rough guide:

DO ADD: Kitchen scraps, tea bags, coffee grounds, wood ash, hair, vacuum cleaner waste, fluff from the tumble dryer, shredded newspaper and cardboard, paper towels, garden prunings and annual weeds.

DON'T ADD: Perennial weeds, diseased plants or roots, woody stems, scraps of meat or fish (which will attract rodents), cat or dog faeces.

SHED

Your shed needs to be sturdy and weather-proof with a door wide enough to get your equipment in and out – including a wheelbarrow – without difficulty. The roof should have a slope so the rainwater can run off, preferably into a downpipe that takes it to a water butt. If the roof is strong and well supported you might like to consider planting up a 'green' roof of sedum or other small plants or bulbs. A well-ordered shed needs plenty of storage. Fit shelves or recycle old bookcases, cupboards or a small chest of drawers to do the job. Tools can be suspended from butcher's hooks fixed to the ceiling or to a baton along one of the walls. Smaller items such as string, labels, gloves, small tools etc can be kept in old jam jars, empty paint tins, or small cardboard boxes. If there's no room for a workbench, consider fitting a drop-down table top to the back of the door, or on the outside.

GREENHOUSE

A greenhouse is extremely useful for extending the season for all crops, but especially tender ones, and for giving you a wider choice of available vegetables during the winter months. Heating can come from a permanent electricity supply or portable heaters, and ventilation is important – you need at least two openers, preferably three, depending on the size of the area. Remember, too, you need to be able to stand up comfortably while inside it. You may need to provide protection during hot summers: you can buy blinds or shade netting, but shade paint will do the job just as well. If finances are tight, it's worth looking out for a secondhand greenhouse for sale, or erecting a 'homemade' one: attach chicken wire to wooden batons to form the walls and cover with plastic sheeting or bubble wrap.

BASIC CARE

Good husbandry will ensure your vegetable garden thrives. Keep it tidy and well-maintained: stay on top of the weeding; leave areas of natural habitat to encourage the beneficial insects (including ladybirds and hoverflies) and natural predators (hedgehogs, frogs, toads and ground beetles) that are your allies against pest and disease; and, of course, keep the soil fertile.

ORGANIC V CHEMICAL

Since one of the primary reasons for growing your own is to avoid eating food that has been subjected to artificial fertilisers and chemical pesticides, it makes sense to go down the organic route. Sometimes you may need to compromise. If you do, use chemicals sparingly and preferably those that will break down into non-toxic compounds. Work with nature when caring for the soil and encourage natural predators with companion planting, an efficient crop-rotation system that controls the spread of disease and by choosing disease-resistant varieties to sow. Feed the soil, not the plant, is the principle behind growing organically. Encourage beneficial soil organisms and nutrients to flourish by digging in or applying as a mulch, garden compost, leafmould, farmyard and green manure.

DIGGING

An important activity, as it gets air into the soil, breaks up compacted soil so roots can penetrate deeper, exposes weed seeds and pests, and is a way of working manure and organic matter into the ground. Heavy soil is best dug over in late autumn to expose the clods to frost, which will break them down. Then, in the spring, break them down further as you dig or rake soil into a finer tilth for sowing and planting. Dig light soils in spring, but avoid very dry conditions when moisture loss is a greater risk.

Before you start, divide your beds into manageable portions so that you don't get overtired or lose heart. Single digging is the norm; double digging may be necessary on very compacted soils.

SINGLE DIGGING: Dig a trench – about 30cm (12in) wide – to the depth of your spade and remove the topsoil to the far end of the plot you are working on. Dig or fork over the soil inside the trench, then add manure and cover it with the soil dug from a second trench. Fork over to mix the soil and manure together. Work across the plot in the same way, filling the last trench with the topsoil from the first one.

DOUBLE DIGGING: Worked in the same way as single digging, except that when you have dug to the depth of your spade, you then fork over the trench to the depth of your fork before adding the manure. This helps drain off compacted soils, improves poor soil and gives deeper-rooted plants a better chance.

NO-DIGGING: A method of regularly applying a thick mulch – about 8cm (3in) deep – to encourage earthworms, build up fertility and improve the structure of the soil. Probably best followed once your soil is in tip-top condition, and you may need to return to digging if you start to get poor yields or inadequate drainage. You will also need to keep a check on soil-borne pests, which are usually revealed by digging.

Mulching

This is the method of covering soil with a layer of organic or non-organic material to conserve moisture, improve structure, encourage worm activity, keep down weeds, insulate soil, add nutrients and protect from pests. Always apply when the soil is warm and moist, never when it's cold and dry.

USE: organic materials: compost; manure; dried lawn cuttings; mushroom compost; straw; leafmould. Non-organic materials: horticultural fleece; polythene sheeting; cardboard; newspaper.

APPLY IN SPRING: After digging to maintain the good conditions created ready for sowing.

APPLY IN LATE SPRING/EARLY SUMMER: Between rows of seeds and plants to keep down weeds and conserve moisture.

APPLY IN SUMMER: Around fruiting vegetables and sprawling plants, such as courgettes, to protect the fruit.

APPLY IN AUTUMN: Around overwintering crops, such as cabbages, to keep soil warm and make lifting easier in frosty weather.

Manures and fertilisers

These are used to replenish the nutrients taken from the soil. Farmyard manure on straw bedding is the option of choice for the nitrogen from the urine. Never use fresh manure – it's full of pathogens, possibly chemicals or hormones. Allow it to rot down first. Heap it onto heavy polythene and cover tops and sides to keep warm; the presence of bright pink brandling worms are the sign that it's ready to use.

Soil that is well dug and manured needs the minimum of fertilisers, but occasionally it may be necessary to give the soil a boost or to improve fruit yields. Nitrogen, phosphorus and potassium are the main components for a healthy soil.

Organic fertilisers include blood, fish and bone, seaweed meal, hoof and horn and rock potash. Apply them as:

BASE DRESSING: Spread or raked into the soil, before planting or sowing, to give plants a good start.

TOP DRESSING: Spread around crops to boost development.

FOLIAR FEED: Sprayed on or watered in to provide extra nutrients.

GREEN MANURE

This is generally a crop of plants sown solely for digging into the soil to improve fertility or soil structure. Plant in an empty bed and dig up before flowering. Chop up with a spade and leave for a few days to die down before digging into the ground, using as a mulch, or turning into a liquid feed. Choose a type based on your soil conditions, the time it takes to mature and the available space you have.

WILL GROW IN SIX TO EIGHT WEEKS: Buckwheat (*Fagopyrum esculentum*); fenugreek (*Trigonella foenum graecum*); mustard (*Sinapsis alba*); phacelia (*Phacelia tanacetifolia*).

SOW IN AUTUMN TO OVERWINTER: Italian ryegrass; (*Lollium multiflorum*); winter tare (*Vicia sativa*); winter beans or broad beans (*Vicia faba*).

LONG TERM – UP TO A YEAR: Alfalfa (*Medicago sativa*); crimson clover (*Trifolium incarnatum*); trefoil (*Medicago lupilina*).

HOT BED

This is a useful addition to your plot, particularly if you don't have a greenhouse. A hot bed is used to bring on early crops or provide extra growing space. Put a good heap of fresh stable or farmyard manure into a wooden frame; pack down, cover and leave for up to two weeks. Turning occasionally can help. Spread a layer of sieved soil on top – approximately 10cm (4in) deep – and cover with a cold frame. Crops that will thrive include early radishes, lettuces, summer cauliflowers, courgettes, marrows and cucumbers. Clear the bed in the autumn and dig into the soil.

WEEDING

Since weeds compete with vegetables for light, water and nutrients, as well as attracting pests and diseases, it's essential to keep them under control. In the first instance, clear the ground thoroughly and, if possible, leave the bed for a few weeks to allow any dormant seeds to germinate before clearing them away, too. Build regular mulching, hoeing and hand-pulling into your routine and never allow weeds to flower. Once removed, add them to the compost heap, but it's probably best not to include perennial weeds. If there is a persistent patch of weeds, cut them down and cover the area with black polythene or heavy duty cardboard. Cover that with a thick layer of compost or manure and leave over winter. Then, cut slits in the polythene and plant vigorous vegetables such as potatoes, onions or squashes, filling the planting hole with compost. Once harvested, with the organic matter dug in, the bed should be relatively weed-free.

WATERING

Underwatering is more common than overwatering. An occasional good heavy watering is of more benefit than several light ones. Stick your fingers down into the soil to test whether it's damp and to discover if water has penetrated the top layer of soil. For best results, water in the evening or early morning and target the water where it's needed. The early stages are critical for all vegetables, but then it varies – vegetables grown for their leaves, for instance, need a lot of water; while the important time for fruiting vegetables is when flowering starts and the fruits appear. For vegetables that need water at the roots, such as beans or squashes, push a flower pot or a cut-off plastic bottle into the soil beside the plant and fill it with water.

Use a fine rose on the watering can for seedlings and aim for the roots on young plants. Good drainage, mulching and underplanting taller varieties will all contribute to keeping moisture in the soil. Fit guttering and downpipes to the shed and/or greenhouse to collect rainwater in butts. You may even want to consider a system of seeper hoses laid through the beds.

SOWING SEEDS

Buy top-quality, disease-resistant varieties, organic if possible, and keep them dry and cool until you're ready to sow them. Never store them in a plastic bag. Don't plant too deeply and sow sparingly, both to save time when thinning out and to avoid disturbing the root system of the seedlings left behind.

OUTSIDE: Use a garden line to mark out a straight row and draw a drill with a hoe or trowel, then plant the seeds to the recommended depth. To sow seeds thinly, empty some into your hand, then gently sprinkle them with the thumb and forefinger of the other hand. Cover over with soil. When sowing large seeds such as marrow or broad beans, put two or three into each hole (this is called station sowing), thinning all but the strongest after they germinate. Small seeds, such as salad greens, can be scattered evenly over a patch (known as 'broadcasting'). Gently rake in all directions to cover them, or sieve a light covering of soil over them. Remember to label the rows and patches.

THINNING OUT: Once they have germinated, tease out unwanted seedlings so the strongest-looking ones are left just clear of each other. Repeat over the following weeks until the seedlings are at the recommended distances apart.

INSIDE: Use a seed or multi-purpose compost and water it before sowing the seeds. Cover to keep warm. Label it. When the seedlings emerge, remove the cover and make sure the compost stays moist, using a fine spray so as not to damage the seedlings.

PRICKING OUT: Thin the seedlings by holding them firmly by the leaves, then ease out using a dibber and transplant into small pots or biodegradable containers for growing on.

HARDEN OFF: Seeds started off under cover need to be 'hardened-off' before planting outside – i.e. acclimatised to the change of temperature. Either transfer the seedlings to a cold frame and leave open for increasing periods during the day as the weather warms up, or move them out during the warmest part of the day, bringing them back under cover at night.

EARTHING UP: This is the method of drawing soil up around the roots of a plant using a rake or hoe. It's essential when growing potatoes to prevent the tubers turning green and poisonous. But is also done to provide support for tall plants such as broccoli and sweetcorn, or to blanch stems, such as trench celery and fennel. Earth up when the soil is moist, clearing weeds as you do so.

TOOLS AND EQUIPMENT

Before you get started on your vegetable garden, you are going to need a basic set of tools. Always buy the best you can afford. Saving money on tools is a false economy. Choose those made from stainless steel with solid wood handles. Never buy unseen, try them out for size and comfort first. It will make a big difference to your workload if they are comfortable to use. Take good care of them, too. Clean off mud and soil after use and wipe them over with a cloth before putting away. Service them regularly and sharpen them as necessary and they'll last you for years.

BASIC SET

SPADE: An essential tool, needed for heavy digging, breaking up clods, moving soil. They come in many different sizes and shapes, which is why you need to try them to find the one that suits you best. Make sure that the tread on the shoulders fits your foot comfortably, too.

FORK: Used for loosening soil and breaking it down, especially after digging, and for lifting plants. The prongs are either round or flat – though if you are only buying one, the latter may be more useful as they do the minimum of damage to tubers when lifting potatoes and other roots.

RAKE: Used for levelling soil, preparing seedbeds, removing stones and debris. Widths vary, but an 8 to 10-tooth rake is adequate for most purposes. It's very important to make sure the weight and balance are right for you, as it's difficult to work with one that's too heavy or cumbersome.

HOE: You will need two types: the Dutch hoe, which has a flat rectangular blade that is used, as you walk backwards, to remove weeds, loosen soil or draw a drill; and the draw or swan-necked hoe, which has a blade at right angles to the handle. This is pulled towards you rather than pushed away, and is useful on heavier soils and for earthing up.

HAND TROWEL AND FORK: The trowel is a versatile tool, but is primarily used for planting. The fork is useful for weeding near plants and loosening soil. They need to be sturdy and well made. They come in different shapes and sizes, so take your time to find the one that's most comfortable for you.

GARDEN LINE: Essential for making sure your rows are straight when planting seeds. You can buy them, or make your own by tying twine to two short canes. For even greater convenience, make them the same width as the beds.

Making a straight drill using a string line

CULTIVATOR: Not essential, but the three to five claw-like prongs are useful for breaking up ground and weeding between plants.

MATTOCK: This is a heavy chisel-bladed hoe, again not essential, but sometimes easier to use on hard ground.

POCKET KNIFE: Invaluable for slitting open bags of compost or manure, cutting twine, taking cuttings, etc.

SHARPENING STONE: Useful to have to keep edges sharp and well maintained.

SECATEURS/SHEARS: For pruning, cutting, keeping things tidy.

OTHERS

WATERING CAN: Chose a sturdy one – plastic or metal – with a capacity of seven to nine litres (1½–2 gallons). You will need two detachable roses – one coarse and one fine – so you can match flow to plant.

WHEELBARROW: For moving large amounts of soil, manure, plants, bags, etc. Again, size and balance is personal and you may find a secondhand one does the job as well.

BUCKET: For holding soil and liquid materials, or moving quantities of stuff around the plot.

CARRYING SHEET OR BAG: Keep nearby while working to save time on trips to the compost heap or shed.

BAMBOO CANES: A selection of various sizes for marking out areas or positions, and providing support for plants, nets and wire.

TWINE: For tying up branches, stems, canes, wires, etc.

GLOVES: Choose a lighter, supple pair for pruning and planting, and a heavy duty pair for messier jobs such as handling prickly and stinging plants.

HORTICULTURAL FLEECE: To protect plants from the cold or pests, or to warm up the ground.

CLOCHES: A variety of different shapes, sizes and materials, including glass, plastic and polyurethane. For covering rows or individual plants – useful if you want to bring forward or extend the growing season, or for warming up the soil prior to sowing or planting.

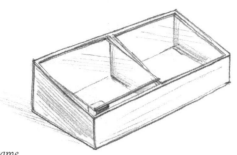

Cold frame

COLD FRAMES: Used for bringing on young plants or protecting a growing crop. They can be static with a solid floor, or movable (without a floor) to offer protection for plants growing in the ground, or adapted to make a hot bed.

FOR SOWING SEEDS

SEED TRAYS AND SMALL POTS: Made of plastic (though wooden and terracotta types also available) and used for sowing seeds that need to be pricked out when they have germinated.

MODULES: For sowing individual seeds to grow on to the planting out stage.

Sowing seeds in plastic pots

BIODEGRADABLE POTS: Used for sowing crops that don't like their roots disturbed. Once the seedling is large enough to be planted out in the ground, the whole thing can go in and the container will rot down as the plant grows.

DIBBER: A pointed metal or wood tool used to make holes for planting seeds or young plants. A small one is used for pricking out seedlings.

LABELS AND MARKER: Essential so you know what's where. Many different types available in plastic, wood or slate with appropriate pencil or pen.

PROPAGATOR LIDS: Usually made of clear plastic and put over seed trays to speed up germination. You could also use cut-off plastic bottles set over individual pots.

ELECTRIC PROPAGATOR: A small unit in which seeds are placed when a specific temperature is needed to germinate them (usually 13–16°C/55–61°F). The heat source may be a light bulb, heated plates or coils. Not essential, but a useful piece of equipment to have and they are usually inexpensive to run.

A YEAR IN THE VEGETABLE PLOT

EARLY SPRING

GENERAL TASKS
- Prepare seedbeds and cover with cloches or black polythene to warm up.
- Check beds are ready for the new season's crops and all weeds and roots have been removed.
- Feed overwintered crops with a general fertiliser or mulch.
- Keep an eye on weeds and watch out for early signs of pests. Cover vulnerable plants with netting or fleece.
- Order seeds and young plants from mail-order companies.
- Check stored vegetables regularly and get rid of any that show signs of deterioration.
- This is the start of the busy season for sowing seeds, pricking out and potting on – check there is plenty of space in cold frames as well as the greenhouse and shed.

TIME TO SOW
IN SITU: American land cress, beetroot, broad beans, carrots, chicory (heading), kohlrabi, peas (earlies), radishes, rocket, spinach, spring onions, turnips.

IN A NURSERY BED: Brussels sprouts (earlies), cabbage (autumn and winter), globe artichokes, leeks, lettuce.

UNDER GLASS: Aubergines, broccoli (calabrese), cauliflowers (summer), chard, celery, okra, onions, peppers, pumpkins, shallots, squashes, indoor tomatoes.

TIME TO PLANT/TRANSPLANT
IN SITU: Asparagus, cabbage (summer), cauliflower (summer),

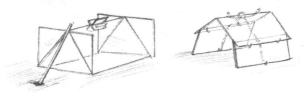

Building a cloche

garlic, globe artichokes, Jerusalem artichokes, onions, potatoes (earlies), shallots.

UNDER GLASS: Early salad leaves, tomatoes.

IN SEASON
American land cress, Brussels sprouts, broccoli (sprouting), cabbages, cauliflowers, celeriac, celery (trench), chard, chicory (forced), lamb's lettuce, leeks, lettuces, parsnips, pumpkins, radishes, rhubarb (forced), spinach, spring onions, swedes, turnip tops.

LATE SPRING

GENERAL TASKS
- Begin to move young plants outside to start the hardening-off process.
- Keep an eye on the soil and water if it becomes very dry. Mulch when the soil is moist to help retain water.
- Hoe regularly to keep on top of weeds and check for signs of pests and disease – especially under cloches or fleece.
- Stay on top of thinning out, earthing up potatoes and providing support for climbers such as peas and beans.
- Clear beds of overwintered vegetables. Store remaining crops and add stumps, roots and any that are not good

enough to keep to the compost heap.
* Prepare beds for new crops: put in supports for netting or wire cages; erect cane supports as required; dig a trench for celery and prepare planting holes for cucurbits.

TIME TO SOW
IN SITU: American land cress, asparagus, beetroot, broad beans, broccoli (calabrese), carrots, chard, chicory (heading and forcing), endive, fennel, kale, kohlrabi, lettuce, onions (bulbing and spring), parsnips, peas, spinach, radishes, rocket, swedes, turnips.

IN A NURSERY BED: Brussels sprouts, cabbages (autumn and winter), cauliflowers (autumn and winter), kale, leeks, broccoli (sprouting).

UNDER GLASS: Beans (borlotti, French and runner), cardoon, courgettes, cucumbers, pumpkins, squashes, sweetcorn, tomatoes (outdoor).

TIME TO PLANT/TRANSPLANT
IN SITU: Asparagus, cabbage (summer), globe artichokes, Jerusalem artichokes, early brassicas, onions, potatoes.

ONCE ALL DANGER OF FROSTS HAS PASSED: Aubergines, celeriac, celery, beans (borlotti, French and runner), peas (earlies), peppers, sweetcorn, tomatoes (outdoor).

UNDER GLASS: Aubergines, cucumbers, tomatoes.

IN SEASON
American land cress, asparagus, broad beans, broccoli (sprouting), Brussels sprouts, cabbages, carrots, cauliflowers, chard, kale, leeks, lettuce, radishes, rhubarb, salad onions, spinach, turnips, turnip tops.

Tying in side shoots

EARLY SUMMER

GENERAL TASKS

- Sow intercrops such as lettuces where there is space. Lightly fork over the ground and add fertiliser first.
- Apply a general fertiliser or high-potash feed to plants that need it, such as squashes, cucumbers and tomatoes.
- Watch for pests and take precautions. Keep on top of watering and weeding.
- Stake, tie in and train sideshoots on crops like beans, cucumbers and tomatoes.
- Order in any seedlings or young plants needed for autumn and winter sowings.
- Start harvesting crops as they are ready.
- It's easy to forget at this time of year to continue with successive sowing to provide a continuous supply of crops. Sow seeds in situ, or under cover for transplanting later.

TIME TO SOW

IN SITU: American land cress, beetroot, cardoon, carrots, chard, chicory (forcing and heading), courgettes, endive (frisée), fennel, kale, kohlrabi, lettuces, peas, radishes, salad onions, spinach, squashes, swedes, sweetcorn, turnips.

IN A NURSERY BED: Winter brassicas.

IN SITU: Beans (borlotti, French and runner), brassicas (autumn and winter), celery, cucumbers, globe artichokes, leeks, lettuces, okra, peppers, pumpkins, squashes, sweetcorn, tomatoes.

IN SEASON
Asparagus, broad beans, broccoli (calabrese), cabbages, carrots, cauliflowers, chard, lamb's lettuce, endive, kohlrabi, American land cress, lettuce, onions (salad and overwintered bulbs), peas, potatoes, radishes, rhubarb, spinach, turnips.

LATE SUMMER

GENERAL TASKS
- Keep picking repeat-producing crops such as beans, courgettes and tomatoes to encourage more to grow.
- Clear away crops that have finished and dig over the ground to expose any pests or weeds in the soil.
- Pests and diseases spread quickly in hot, dry weather, so stay vigilant. If it's wet and humid, watch for potato blight, which thrives in those conditions.
- If you have suitable space, plant up a green manure crop.
- Clear cold frames and the greenhouse ready for sowing and growing winter crops that need protection from frosts.
- Weed, mulch and water.

TIME TO SOW
IN SITU: American land cress, beetroot, carrots, chard, chicory (heading), Chinese cabbage, lamb's lettuce, endive (broad-leaved), fennel, kohlrabi, lettuce, mizuna greens, onions (bulbing and salad), pak choi, peas (autumn), radishes (summer and winter), spinach (winter), turnips.

IN A NURSERY BED: Cabbage (spring and red varieties), kale.
TIME TO PLANT/TRANSPLANT
IN SITU: Broccoli (sprouting), cabbages (spring), cauliflowers (autumn and winter), kale, leeks.

IN SEASON
American land cress, aubergines, beetroot, borlotti beans, broad beans, broccoli (calabrese), cabbage, carrots, cauliflowers, celery, chard, lamb's lettuce, cucumbers, endive, French beans, garlic, globe artichokes, kohlrabi, leeks, lettuce, onions (bulbing), potatoes, radishes, runner beans, salad onions, shallots, spinach, squashes, sweetcorn, tomatoes, turnips.

EARLY AUTUMN

GENERAL TASKS
- Cover late and overwintering crops with cloches or fleeces if the weather turns cold.
- Clear spent crops and supports from beds ready for autumn digging and liming.
- Cover root vegetables that are being left in the ground with straw, or lift and store in a frost-free place.
- Start gathering together used pots, seed trays, labels, canes etc and clean and store ready for future use.

TIME TO SOW
IN SITU: Broad beans, carrots, peas, rocket, spinach (winter).

IN A NURSERY BED: Cabbages (spring), cauliflowers (summer).

UNDER GLASS: Lettuces, mizuna greens, pak choi, radishes.

TIME TO PLANT/TRANSPLANT
IN SITU: Cabbages (spring), garlic, onions (autumn).

UNDER GLASS: Lettuces.

IN SEASON
Aubergines, beetroot, broccoli (calabrese and sprouting),
Brussels sprouts, cabbages, cardoons, carrots, cauliflowers,
celeriac, celery, chicory (heading), cucumbers, endive, fennel,
French beans, Jerusalem artichokes, kale, kohlrabi, leeks,
lettuces, mizuna greens, okra, onions, pak choi, parsnips,
peas, peppers, potatoes, pumpkins, radishes, runner beans,
spinach, squashes, swedes, sweetcorn, tomatoes, turnips.

LATE AUTUMN

GENERAL TASKS
- Clear all non-hardy crops and dig over the ground. If it's
  heavy leave clods on top to allow the frost to break it down.
- Lift and store any remaining winter crops that are at risk of
  severe weather. Check any stored crops are still in good
  condition.
- Earth up stems of cabbages, cauliflowers and Brussels
  sprouts to protect from wind rock.
- Gather leaves together to make your own nutritious
  leafmould to use as a mulch (it should be ready in a year).
  Erect a simple structure of wire netting wrapped around
  three or four stakes and pile in the leaves, pushing down
  firmly. Or pack them into black plastic bags, punch in a
  few holes and leave to rot down – this may take longer
  than a year.

TIME TO SOW
IN SITU: Broad beans, carrots, peas.

UNDER GLASS: Lettuces, mizuna greens, pak choi, radishes, rocket.

TIME TO PLANT/TRANSPLANT
IN SITU: Cabbages (spring), garlic, onions (autumn).

IN SEASON
American land cress, Brussels sprouts, cabbages, carrots, cauliflowers, celeriac, celery, chard, chicory (heading and forced), Chinese cabbage, lamb's lettuce, endive, fennel, kohlrabi, Jerusalem artichokes, kale, leeks, lettuce, mizuna greens, okra, pak choi, parsnips, potatoes, pumpkins, radishes, rhubarb, spinach, swedes, turnips.

WINTER

GENERAL TASKS
- Carry on with digging and preparing soil as weather permits.
- Continue to check stored crops regularly for signs of mould, pests or diseases.
- Clean cloches and cold frames that aren't in use.
- If bad weather is forecast, lift a supply of fresh vegetables so you don't need to do so in the snow or frost.
- Check compost bins: empty them out, mix the contents together, then refill.
- Put out cloches, cold frames, black polythene or straw to warm up beds ready for early plantings.
- Clean and sharpen tools for the start of the new gardening year. Check over equipment – including sundry items such as seed trays, canes, labels, string etc – replacing or supplementing where needed.

- On a fine day, walk round your plot to remind yourself of the year's successes and failures, making notes if necessary, to help plan next year's crops and rotations. Order in seeds and young plants.

TIME TO SOW

UNDER GLASS: Aubergine, beetroot, broad beans, cabbages (summer), carrots, cauliflowers (summer), celeriac, celery, cucumbers, leeks, lettuces, onions, radishes, salad onions, spinach.

TIME TO PLANT/TRANSPLANT

IN SITU: Garlic, globe artichokes, rhubarb, shallots.

IN SEASON

American land cress, broccoli (sprouting), Brussels sprouts, cabbages, carrots, cauliflowers, celeriac, celery, chicory (forced and heading), lamb's lettuce, endive, fennel, Jerusalem artichokes, kale, kohlrabi, leeks, lettuces, mizuna greens, pak choi, parsnips, radishes, rhubarb (forced), spinach, swedes.

VEGETABLE VARIETIES
ROOT VEGETABLES

Although specific needs may vary, all root vegetables need a stone-free, well-cultivated, moisture-retentive soil to grow straight roots. Mostly they are sown in situ as they don't transplant well. You need to get the water balance right – too much and they will produce more leaf than root; allowing them to dry out and then giving them a good soaking can mean the roots will fork or the plant bolt. Potatoes can be planted on their own as part of the rotation system, or used to 'clear' poor ground.

BEETROOT (*Beta vulgaris*)

Beetroot are usually red, but there are also yellow, white and multicoloured varieties. Choose bolt-resistant varieties for early sowings in spring. Dig over plot in autumn or early winter, adding well-rotted compost or lime if the soil is acid.

SOWING: For early crops, sow under cover from late winter in modules, then harden-off and plant out in clusters 30–38cm (12–15in) apart. For main crops, sow outdoors from late spring, in full sun, at four-weekly intervals until late summer before autumn frosts set in. Sow 2cm (¾in) deep 2.5cm (1in) apart, in rows 23–30cm (9–12in) apart. Monogerm types produce single seedlings, so don't need thinning.

GROWING: Thin out to 10cm (4in) apart and weed carefully so as not to injure roots. Avoid overwatering, which will cause more leaves to be produced, but don't allow to dry out or the roots will toughen. Mulch well to keep in moisture.

PESTS AND DISEASES: Tendency to bolt. Cutworm.

HARVESTING: Ready in 8–16 weeks. For earlies or baby beets, lift when golf-ball-size, maincrops should be the size of tennis balls. Cut off foliage, loosen the soil with a fork and lift carefully. Store autumn crops in moist sand in a cool shed or leave in the ground under a covering of straw.

CARROT (Daucus carota)

Divided into two groups – earlies and late or maincrop – carrots are usually orange or red, but purple, yellow and white varieties are also available. With successive sowing, you can have fresh carrots for much of the year. Choose a warm sheltered site for earlies, while maincrop do better in an open site. The soil should be light, well-drained and free of stones. Dig in plenty of organic matter some months before planting as they don't do well in freshly manured ground.

SOWING: Once the ground has started to warm up in early spring, sow seeds thinly in drills 1–2cm (½–¾in) deep under cloches or cold frames, in rows 15cm (6in) apart. For a succession of carrots, continue sowing a few seeds every two weeks from mid-spring to mid-summer. For winter crop sow in late summer/late autumn.

GROWING: For earlies, thin to 8–10cm (3–4in) apart, maincrop to 5–8cm (2–3in). Weed carefully (the smell will alert carrot fly) and mulch between rows to retain moisture. Avoid excessive watering – just enough to keep soil moist.

PESTS AND DISEASES: Carrot fly, cutworm.

COMPANION PLANTING: Marigolds (tagetes) help confuse carrot fly, but choose a strong-smelling variety. A crop of onions, leeks or chives may also work.

HARVESTING: Earlies ready in 7–10 weeks; maincrop, 10–16 weeks. Pull out by hand if soil is light; you may need to use a fork if the soil is heavy. To store, lift, twist off foliage and store in boxes of sand in a cool, dry place.

JERUSALEM ARTICHOKE (*Helianthus tuberosus*)

Related to the sunflower, the Jerusalem artichoke makes a good screen or windbreak as it grows to 3m (10ft). Although they are perennials, they should be treated as annuals otherwise they become weedy.

SOWING: Happy in any soil, sun or shade, provided it's not very acid or prone to waterlogging. Plant tubers in early spring 10cm (4in) deep, 30cm (12in) apart.

GROWING: Earth-up when plants reach about 30cm (12in) and stake to offer support. Water when dry. Remove any flower buds as soon as they appear.

PEST AND DISEASES: Slugs may attack the tubers.

HARVESTING: Ready in 26 weeks. Once leaves turn brown in autumn, cut down the stems. Protect the area with straw if very cold and dig up the tubers as needed during the winter. In early spring, clear the site completely, keeping a few healthy tubers for replanting.

PARSNIP (*Pastinaca sativa*)

A reliable winter crop that benefits from a good frost, which improves the flavour. Plant lettuces or radishes between the rows as an intercrop. Germination can be slow, so if sowing directly outside, cover the plot up to a week before to warm up the soil.

Bottomless plastic bottles protect young plants

SOWING: Parsnips enjoy similar conditions to carrots. You can start them off in biodegradable modules under glass, or sow directly into the ground once it has warmed up. Sow in drills 2.5cm (1in) deep, 30cm (12in) apart; or sow three seeds in stations 12.5cm (5in) apart.

GROWING: When 5cm (2in) high, thin to the strongest seedling. Weed regularly and never allow to get dry. Mulch to retain moisture.

PESTS AND DISEASES: Carrot fly and parsnip canker.

COMPANION PLANTING: Marigolds (tagetes) help confuse carrot fly.

HARVESTING: Ready in 20–35 weeks. When the leaves die down in autumn, leave in the ground for the frosts to sweeten them. Use a fork to lift as needed, protecting with straw if very cold. Remove and store any still remaining at the end of February and clear the ground.

POTATOES *(Solanum tuberosum)*

A good crop to plant if the ground is poor, as the roots help break down the soil and all the digging and earthing-up required help turn it over. Generally, plant earlies for new potatoes in summer and maincrop for winter storage. For 'new' potatoes in early winter, plant earlies in a bucket or a

Chitting potatoes

sheltered spot in late summer. Buy disease-resistant seed potatoes from a quality source. Never plant next to tomatoes, as they can pass disease between each other. Potatoes prefer an open, sunny plot in well-drained, well-manured soil. Delay planting if the conditions are cold and wet.

SOWING: Start off seed potatoes by 'chitting'. Place them in egg boxes or wooden trays, with the 'eyes' facing upwards and leave in a warm, light place out of direct sunlight. After about six weeks, when the shoots are around 2.5cm (1in) long, they're ready for planting out.

GROWING: Plant 10–15cm (4–6in) deep.

Set earlies 30cm (12in) apart, with 45cm (18in) between rows. Set maincrops 38cm (15in) apart, with 75cm (30in) between rows. Cover with soil. When the stalks are about 23cm (9in) high, start earthing-up. Half-cover them with soil, and repeat every three weeks for maincrops until the leaves at the top meet (this is to prevent tubers turning green). Keep moist, watering earlies regularly and maincrops when flowers form and in dry weather.

PESTS AND DISEASES: Potato cyst eelworm, slugs, wireworm, cutworm and potato blight.

HARVESTING: Earlies ready in 12–14 weeks. 2nd-earlies: 15–18 weeks. Maincrops: 18–22 weeks. Lift as the stalks die down. Store in a dark, frost-free place.

LEGUMES

All legumes need a well-dug, well-drained soil that is slightly alkaline. Dig over in autumn and add plenty of compost or well-rotted manure. An acid soil will need to be limed. The roots carry nodules that are a good source of nitrogen; once the plants have finished producing, cut off at ground level and leave the roots to rot down and enrich the soil. They have a long cropping season, as the more you pick, the more will grow. They can also be dried and stored for winter use.

RUNNER BEANS (Phaseolus coccineus)

Runner beans need space for a good root run, in a sunny, sheltered spot. Before planting, erect a framework of supporting canes – they can grow up to 3m (10ft).

SOWING: Start off under cover in biodegradable pots or root trainers and move outside in May or June when all danger of frosts has passed. To sow seeds in situ, make a v-shaped trench 5cm (2in) deep and sow seeds 15cm (6in) apart, with 60cm (24in) between rows.

GROWING: Hoe regularly to keep down weeds, mulch to preserve moisture and water regularly. Loosely tie in young plants. Pinch out tips when plants reach 60cm (2ft) high, then again at 1.2m (4ft).

PESTS AND DISEASES: Slugs, snails and mice.

HARVESTING: Ready in 12–16 weeks. Pick every few days once pods reach 15–20cm (6–8in) long and before they start to swell. Check for pods hidden in the foliage as if left they will inhibit production.

FRENCH BEANS (*Phaseolus vulgaris*)

Usually eaten when young. If left they become flageolets, then haricot beans and can be dried and stored. You can get either climbing or dwarf varieties, in different colours, with flat or pointed pods. They need a light, rich soil in a sunny sheltered position. Never sow when cold or soil is wet.

SOWING: Sow indoors, in pots 4–5cm (1½–2in) deep, a month before the last frosts. Transfer outside in late spring or early summer, or sow directly into the ground: station-sow two seeds in drills 5cm (2in) deep, 15–23cm (6–9in) apart, in rows 60cm (24in) apart.

GROWING: Provide wigwam canes as support for climbers, tie in young shoots. Protect with fleece if there's a sudden cold snap. Keep moist and well mulched, especially after flowering. Pinch out tips when climbers reach 60cm (2ft) high, then again at 1.2m (4ft). Support dwarf varieties with a layer of twiggy sticks.

PESTS AND DISEASES: Slugs, birds, mice, black bean aphid/blackfly.

Wigwam supports for beans

COMPANION PLANTING: Poached egg plant (limnanthes) will attract hoverflies, which feed on aphids.

HARVESTING: Ready in 8–12 weeks. Pick when pods are about 15cm (6in) long. Pick regularly to prolong cropping. If leaving to mature, wait till the pods start to wither, then pick, dry and store in an airtight container.

PEAS *(Pisum sativum)*

Grow in a rich, moisture-retentive soil in full sun or slight shade, allowing for a good root run. The round-seeded varieties are used for early sowings and overwintering, the wrinkled ones for maincrop and successional sowings, sown from early spring till midsummer at 3–4 week intervals. Never sow when cold or wet.

SOWING: Sow in modules under cover, harden off and transplant when ground has warmed up. Sow directly into the soil from late spring. Use a hoe to create a drill and space seeds 8–20cm (3–4in) apart, with 45cm (18in) between rows. Continue sowing every few weeks for a succession throughout the summer. Sow in July for an autumn crop.

Flower pot pushed into soil beside beans enables water to reach roots quicker

GROWING: As soon as shoots appear, provide support and protection from birds. Hoe regularly and mulch to retain moisture. Water well, especially when flowers appear.

PESTS: Birds, slugs, mice, aphids, pea moth, powdery mildew.

COMPANION PLANTING: Try a 'sacrifice' plant such as nasturtiums to attract aphids away from the crop, or a hedge of lavender or rosemary.

HARVESTING: Ready in 12–16 weeks; autumn-sown take 30–34 weeks to mature. Start testing whether pods are ready when they look heavy, then pick regularly, holding the stem firmly as you do so. Once harvested, leave the nitrogen-rich roots in the soil.

MANGETOUT AND SUGARSNAP PEAS (*Pisum sativum*)

Sow and grow in the same way as ordinary peas, but pick and eat whole before the seeds swell. Ready in 8–10 weeks, when pods snap easily in half.

BROAD BEANS (*Vicia faba*)

Very hardy and easy to grow, the flowers have a heady scent. Unlike other legumes, broad beans are happy in a clay soil.

SOWING: Sow in late winter or early spring at monthly intervals for a continuous crop. Start off in modules or seed trays for the first sowings or in a piece of guttering from which you can slide off the young plants directly into the seed trench, or plant directly into the soil, 5cm (2in) deep. Space 23cm (9in) apart in staggered rows, set 75cm (30in) apart.

GROWING: Earth up tall varieties. Support with canes either individually, or with wire or bean netting attached to canes positioned along the rows. Mulch and don't allow to dry out. Pinch off tips when plants are flowering to encourage pods to form and discourage blackfly.

PESTS AND DISEASES: Black bean aphid/blackfly; mice; chocolate spot.

COMPANION PLANTING: Poached egg plant (limnanthes) will attract hoverflies, which feed on aphids. Nasturtiums or borage to attract blackfly away from the crop.

HARVESTING: Ready in 12–15 weeks. Pick when pods are about 5–8cm (2–3in) long to eat whole, or, for the beans, as soon as the seed shape is visible through the pod. Broad beans are prolific – the more you pick, the more they will grow.

SOMETHING DIFFERENT

BORLOTTI BEANS (*Phaseolus vulgaris*)

With pretty, mottled red pods and large tasty beans, borlotti beans feature highly in Italian dishes and can be used fresh or dried. They produce 6–7 beans per pod and grow up to about 1m (3ft 3in) high. Dwarf as well as climber varieties available.

SOWING: Sow indoors, in pots 4–5cm (1½–2in) deep, a month before the last frosts. Transfer outside in late spring or early summer, or sow directly into the ground: station-sow two seeds in drills 5cm (2in) deep, 15–23cm (6–9in) apart, in rows 60cm (24in) apart.

GROWING: Provide wigwam canes or netting as support for climbers, tie in young shoots. Protect with fleece if there's a cold snap. Keep moist and well mulched, especially after flowering. Pinch out tips when climbers reach 60cm (2ft) high, then again at 1.2m (4ft). Support dwarf varieties with a layer of sticks.

PESTS: Slugs, birds, mice, black bean aphid/blackfly.

COMPANION PLANTING: Poached egg plant (limnanthes) will attract hoverflies, which feed on aphids.

HARVESTING: Ready in 12 weeks. Pick once the pods start to turn red. If you want to dry beans for winter, leave a few plants unpicked until late summer when the pods are hard and the beans rattle. Shell, dry thoroughly and store in an airtight jar or tin in a cool, dry place.

BRASSICAS

All brassicas need a fertile (but not too rich), well-drained soil. Dig over well, add compost and then leave for several months to settle down before planting: brassicas need firm ground or they become subject to wind rock. Lime the soil if it's too acid. They prefer cold weather and will often bolt in very hot conditions. Brassicas (except those grown for their roots) are best started off in a nursery bed under cloches or in modules. A word of warning, however – the seedlings are very similar so, to avoid any surprises, label clearly! Always firm-in thoroughly when transferring to the permanent bed. As leafy vegetables, they need to be watered well during dry weather.

KALE OR BORECOLE (*Brassica oleracea/Acephala Group*)

Very hardy, easy to grow and does well in poor soils. A good source of winter greens, the curly-leaved variety is ready in the autumn, the plain-leaved from late winter. A frost is said to improve the flavour.

Asparagus

Beetroot

Broad bean

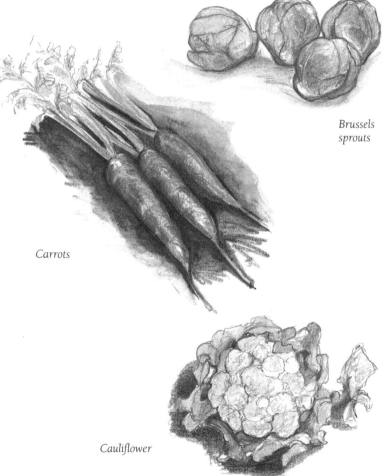

Brussels sprouts

Carrots

Cauliflower

SOWING: Sow in situ from mid to late spring in drills 1cm (½in) deep. Thin to 45cm (18in) apart.

GROWING: Keep well watered, remove yellowing leaves and support stems as needed. Earth up taller varieties in autumn to protect against wind rock.

PESTS AND DISEASES: Usually trouble free.

HARVESTING: Ready in 26–40 weeks. Pick while the leaves are young and tender, older leaves tend to be bitter. Work outwards from the crown to encourage side shoots to form.

CAULIFLOWERS *(Brassica oleracea/Botrytis Group)*

Cauliflowers need a rich, deep soil, no wind and regular watering to succeed. Summer and autumn crops grow in one season, while winter varieties can take up to a year.

SOWING: Start off early summer varieties under glass in late winter; sow in modules, harden off and transplant outside in early spring 45cm (18in) apart, with 60cm (24in) between rows. Sow autumn and winter crops in late spring and transplant to the main bed 6 weeks later. Sow all varieties successively to have a continuous harvest.

GROWING: Hoe regularly and keep well watered. Feed occasionally. Turn the leaves over the developing heads to protect from sun or frost.

PESTS AND DISEASES: Birds, clubroot, cutworm.

HARVESTING: Summer varieties ready in 16–20 weeks; winter, 40–50 weeks. Cut while the heads are young and firm, leaving some leaves on to protect the curds. To store, hang upside down in a cool, frost-free place. Spray regularly to keep moist.

CABBAGE *(Brassica oleracea/Capitata Group)*

There are spring, summer, autumn and winter varieties, providing cabbage all year round. All are grown in the same way. Sow successively to provide a staggered harvest.

SOWING: To start off under glass, sow in seed trays or modules, prick out and transplant to permanent position when seedlings have three to four true leaves. Use a dibber when planting out and firm the soil round them well. If sowing in situ, sow in a furrow, 10cm (4in) deep, thinning to required space. Fill in the furrow as the plant grows.

Summer varieties: sow under cover in early spring and transplant to main bed in late spring, spacing plants 35–45cm (12–18in) apart.

Autumn and winter varieties: sow under cover in mid to late spring, transplanting in early summer, spacing plants 50cm (20in) apart.

Spring varieties: sow in situ from mid to late summer, in rows 30cm (12in) apart, thinning seedlings to 10–15cm (4–6in) apart for 'greens', 30cm (12in) for heads.

GROWING: Water generously once heads form and remove dead leaves regularly. Earth up the base of the plants to protect from frosts. Don't fertilise during the winter.

PESTS AND DISEASES: Birds, slugs, snails, cabbage white butterflies, cabbage root fly, clubroot, mealy aphids, flea beetle, cutworm.

COMPANION PLANTING: Clover has been known to deter cabbage root fly.

HARVESTING: Spring varieties ready in 20–35 weeks; summer varieties, 20 weeks; autumn varieties, 26–30 weeks; winter varieties, 30–35 weeks. Cut young leaves as needed for 'greens'. Cut heads close to the ground. Spring and early summer varieties will produce a second cluster of smaller heads if you cut a cross about 1cm (½in) deep in the stump left in the ground. Winter and red varieties can be lifted and stored, packed loosely in straw. Clear the ground completely once the harvest is over.

BRUSSELS SPROUTS (Brassica oleracea/Gemmifera Group)

Different varieties will give you crops from early autumn to mid spring.

SOWING: Sow a succession of early, maincrop and late sowings at two-weekly intervals. Thin out to 15cm (6in) apart and transplant when about 23cm (9in) high into square rows 60cm (24in) apart.

GROWING: Hoe regularly, keep well watered in dry spells. In autumn earth up and stake if windy. Regularly remove any yellowing leaves.

PESTS AND DISEASES: Birds, caterpillars, mealy aphids, cutworm.

HARVESTING: Ready in 20–36 weeks. Pick from the bottom of the stalk when they're still tightly closed, snapping them off cleanly and removing any leaves. The stem tops can be cooked as 'greens'. At the end of the season, dig up and clear the plot.

BROCCOLI (*Brassica oleracea/Italica Group*)

There are three main types of broccoli, all sown in spring and planted out in summer – calabrese is harvested in autumn, purple and white sprouting varieties in spring.

SOWING: Calabrese doesn't like its roots disturbed, so plant in modules or outside in situ in stations and thin when seedlings appear. Plant out sprouting varieties 60cm (24in) apart in a square with 30–40cm (12–18in) between rows.

GROWING: Keep weed free, water regularly and mulch. Earth up in autumn and provide support for stems in windy positions.

PESTS AND DISEASES: Pigeons in winter, caterpillars, cutworm.

HARVESTING: Ready in 40 weeks. Pick before flowering. Cut the stem first, then the side shoots when they're 10–13cm (4–5in) long.

The following, while strictly members of the brassica family as they prefer the same type of soil and are vulnerable to the same pests and diseases, are more usually grown for their roots.

SWEDE (*Brassica napus/Napobrassica Group*)

Closely related to the turnip, the swede is hardier and the flesh is usually yellow. An autumn/winter vegetable that needs a moist, fertile soil.

SOWING: Sow from late spring to early summer, 2cm (¾in) deep in drills. Thin until final spacing is 23cm (9in) apart, with 38cm (15in) between rows.

GROWING: Keep well weeded and water regularly – don't allow to dry out.

PESTS AND DISEASES: Seedlings vulnerable to flea beetle, cabbage root fly and mealy cabbage aphid; the mature plant to clubroot and powdery mildew.

HARVESTING: Ready in 20–26 weeks. Lift as required during autumn and mid winter. Cover with straw, or lift, twist off the leaves and store in boxes between layers of moist sand in a cool, frost-free place.

TURNIP *(Brassica rapa/Rapifera Group)*

Early varieties can be round, flat or cylindrical in shape, while maincrop tend to be round. The flesh is either white or yellow. They need a moist, fertile soil.

SOWING: Sow thinly in drills 2.5cm (1in) deep, in rows 23cm (9in) apart, every three or four weeks from early spring to late summer. Thin out to 10cm (6in) apart. Sow maincrop varieties in late summer for autumn eating; thin out to 20cm (8in) apart. Sow in autumn to harvest the leafy tops in March.

GROWING: Keep weed-free and evenly moist as irregular watering causes the roots to split.

PESTS AND DISEASES: The usual brassica pests and diseases, particularly flea beetle; slugs and snails may attack seedlings.

HARVESTING: Ready in 6–12 weeks. Pull early crops when they're roughly the size of a golf ball; maincrops when they're as big as a tennis ball. Store maincrops over winter in a cool frost-free place, packed into a box between layers of moist sand. If growing for the leafy tops in March, cover with a high ridge of soil in late winter.

RADISH (*Raphanus sativus*)

There are two varieties of radish, summer and winter, and both do well in a fertile, moisture-retentive soil.

SOWING: Sow seeds thinly 1cm (½in) deep in rows 15cm (6in) apart. Sow successively, every few weeks, for a continuous supply throughout the season. If necessary, thin to about 4cm (2in) between seedlings. Sow winter radishes in rows 25cm (10in) apart, thinned to 10cm (4in) apart.

GROWING: Water and weed regularly.

PESTS AND DISEASES: Flea beetle, slugs, snails, birds. If left in the ground too long, at risk of cabbage root fly.

HARVESTING: The summer radish is ready in 4 weeks; the winter radish, 10–12 weeks. Pull summer radishes as needed; winter radishes can be left in the ground, covered with straw and lifted as required. To store, lift, twist off foliage and store in boxes of moist sand in a cool, dry place.

SOMETHING DIFFERENT
KOHLRABI (*Brassica oleracea/Gongyloides group*)

A form of kale grown for its swollen stem, so it doesn't need a deep soil to thrive.

SOWING: Sow every few weeks from early spring (protected by cloches) to late summer. Sow 1cm (½in) deep in rows 30cm (12in) apart. Thin seedlings as first true leaves appear, aiming for a final spacing of 23cm (9in).

GROWING: Weed regularly and keep well watered.

PESTS AND DISEASES: May need protection from aphids and birds.

COMPANION PLANTING: Any 'sacrifice' plant to attract aphids away from the crop.

HARVESTING: Ready in 8–10 weeks. Dig up when the stems are the size of a tennis ball. Late sowings can be left in the ground until December. They do not store well.

PAK CHOI (*Brassica rapa* var. *chinensis*)

Closely related to the Chinese cabbage, all parts of the plant can be eaten. Varieties differ in height from 8–10cm (3–4in) to 45cm (18in). Look for bolt-resistant varieties.

SOWING: Sow seeds in situ 1cm (½in) deep, in rows 30cm (12in) apart, every few weeks for a continuous crop. Thin according to the size you want: small, 15cm (6in) apart; medium 18cm (7in) apart; large 35cm (14in) apart. Sow under cover in autumn for a winter crop.

GROWING: Keep weed free and water well.

PESTS AND DISEASES: All the usual brassica predators: birds, slugs, snails, cabbage white butterflies, cabbage root fly, clubroot, mealy aphids, cutworm, flea beetle.

HARVESTING: Ready in 3 weeks. Pick leaves as needed, leaving the plant in the ground to resprout.

MIZUNA GREENS (*Brassica rapa* var. *nipposinica*)

Grow as a cut-and-come-again crop. Will benefit from some protection from the sun in high summer.

SOWING: Sow thinly in drills from mid summer, thinning out to about 15cm (6in) apart. Sow under cover in autumn for a winter crop.

GROWING: Keep weed free and well watered. Net to protect from pests.

PESTS AND DISEASES: All the usual brassica predators: birds, slugs, snails, cabbage white butterflies, cabbage root fly, clubroot, mealy aphids, cutworm, flea beetle.

HARVESTING: Ready in 3 weeks. Pick leaves as needed, leaving the plant in the ground to resprout.

CHINESE CABBAGE *(Brassica rapa* var. *perkinensis)*

Needs a very fertile soil and plenty of water to succeed. Don't sow too early in the year or it will bolt. Wait until after mid-summer.

SOWING: As they dislike being disturbed, sow seeds in situ 1cm (½in) deep, in rows 30cm (12in) apart, every few weeks for a continuous crop. Or start off in biodegradable pots for transplanting later.

GROWING: Weed regularly, mulch and keep well watered. Net to protect from pests.

PESTS AND DISEASES: All the usual brassica predators: birds, slugs, snails, cabbage white butterflies, cabbage root fly, clubroot, mealy aphids, cutworm, flea beetle.

HARVESTING: Ready in 6–10 weeks. Cut when the heads are solid and before the first frosts. Can be stored in a cool, frost-free place.

THE ONION FAMILY

All members of the onion family like a well-drained, fertile plot. If the soil is very acid, apply a layer of lime in autumn and dig in plenty of compost. Do not plant in a freshly manured spot. They need an open, sunny site that is kept weed free. Their distinctive flowers are very attractive to bees and can also be cut and dried – you may like to consider growing some just for their flowers if you have the space.

ONIONS *(Allium cepa)*

Maincrop varieties are sown in spring for harvesting in autumn and overwinter storage; the Japanese varieties are sown in late summer/early autumn for harvesting the following summer.

SOWING: Sow seed under glass and prick out into modules for transplanting, or sow in situ in late spring. Sow thinly 1cm (½in) deep, in rows 30cm (12in) apart. Thin in stages until they are 10cm (4in) apart. Or sow as small bulbs (onion sets): bury the bulbs in the ground so the tip just shows, 10cm (4in) apart, with 30cm (12in) between rows.

GROWING: It's important to keep the site weed-free. Mulch to retain moisture. Water and feed spring-sown onions until midsummer, then water only if they start to wilt. Feed overwintered bulbs once in early spring, cover with fleece to protect from frost if bulbs start to lift from the soil.

PESTS AND DISEASES: Birds, onion fly, onion white rot, onion neck rot, onion eelworm. Sets are usually less prone to disease.

COMPANION PLANTING: A 'sacrifice' crop of carrots alongside may confuse the onion fly.

HARVESTING: Spring-sown ready in 16–22 weeks; overwintered, 40–46 weeks. Once the tops have turned over and died down, lift carefully with a fork and leave on top of the soil to dry out if the weather's good, bring indoors if it's wet. Plait into strings, tie in nets, or lay in a single layer in a box and store in a frost-free place.

SPRING (SALAD) ONIONS *(Allium cepa)*

Also known as bunching onions or scallions, they are fast-growing and can be used as an intercrop between larger-growing varieties or between carrots as a companion plant.

SOWING: Sow in drills every three to four weeks from early spring to late summer. Space seeds about 3cm (1¼in) apart with 15cm (6in) between rows. There is no need to thin further.

GROWING: Keep weed-free and water in dry conditions.

PESTS AND DISEASES: Birds, onion fly, onion white rot, onion neck rot, onion eelworm.

COMPANION PLANTING: A 'sacrifice' crop of carrots alongside may confuse the onion fly.

HARVESTING: Ready in 8–10 weeks. As soon as they reach a reasonable size, pull alternate plants as needed.

SHALLOTS (*Allium cepa/Aggregatum group*)

Shallots have a very distinctive flavour and are easy to grow, but need a longer time in the ground than onions.

SOWING: Sow seed indoors in early spring, then plant outside in late spring, 15cm (6in) apart with 23–30cm (9–12in) between rows. Plant sets in situ in late winter (traditionally the shortest day), with the tips just showing, 15cm (6in) apart with 23–30cm (9–12in) between rows.

GROWING: It's important to keep the site weed-free. Mulch to retain moisture. Water and feed spring-sown onions until midsummer, then water only if they start to wilt. Feed overwintered bulbs once in early spring, cover with fleece to protect from frost if bulbs start to lift from the soil.

PESTS AND DISEASES: Birds, onion fly, onion white rot, onion neck rot, onion eelworm. Sets are usually less prone to disease.

COMPANION PLANTING: A 'sacrifice' crop of carrots alongside may confuse the onion fly.

HARVESTING: Ready in 26 weeks. Lift when the leaves die down, leave to dry out, then store as for onions. Healthy bulbs can be saved for replanting the following season.

LEEKS (*Allium porrum*)

Early varieties are ready to harvest in late summer, maincrops in the winter, and lates in spring. They need a moist soil with plenty of humus; good drainage is essential for maincrops.

SOWING: Start seed off under glass: earlies in late winter, maincrops in spring and lates in early summer. When seedlings are 20cm (8in) tall they're ready to transplant. Harden off, then make a 15cm (6in) deep hole with a dibber where they are to grow and drop in the young plant. Space 15cm (6in) apart with 30cm (12in) between rows.

GROWING: Keep weed-free, water regularly and mulch. Earth up in stages to keep the stems white, taking care to avoid getting soil between the leaves. Cover maincrops and lates with cloches during cold weather.

PESTS AND DISEASES: Birds, onion fly, onion white rot, onion neck rot, onion eelworm, leek rust.

COMPANION PLANTING: A 'sacrifice' crop of carrots alongside may confuse the onion fly.

HARVESTING: Ready in 26–40 weeks. Lift carefully as required. If you need the space, lift what's left in the ground and heel-in in a spare plot where they'll keep fresh for a few weeks.

GARLIC (*Allium sativum*)

Needs plenty of sunshine to grow. Do not plant in freshly manured soil, but you could add potash before planting. Buy bulbs from a reputable nursery or seed merchant, never use those bought from a supermarket or greengrocer.

SOWING: Plant the cloves from late autumn to late winter in situ. Using a dibber, push the pointed end in to the soil to a depth of 7.5–10cm (3–4in) leaving just the tip showing. Space them 10cm (4in) apart, with 30cm (12in) between rows.

GROWING: Keep weed-free, water during spring and early summer, then only when very dry.

PESTS AND DISEASES: Usually trouble free, but may be affected by mould or rust, or onion white rot. May need protection from birds when first planted.

HARVESTING: Ready in 24–36 weeks. When the leaves turn yellow, dig them up carefully and dry as for onions. Store in a cool, frost-free place. Healthy bulbs can be saved for replanting.

THE PUMPKIN FAMILY *(Cucurbits)*

Cucurbits prefer a slightly acid soil, in a sunny, sheltered, well-drained spot. The soil needs to be humus-rich, so dig in plenty of well-rotted compost – they will grow well on a manure or compost heap. They produce both male and female flowers; you will need to remove any covering to allow insects to pollinate them. The flowers, as well as the fruit, are edible.

COURGETTES AND MARROWS *(Cucurbita pepo)*

Courgettes are the young fruit of marrows. Bush or trailing varieties include round or long fruits in green or yellow. Prepare the ground prior to planting by digging a hole to a spade's depth and mixing the excavated soil with a bucket of well-rotted manure or compost. Refill the hole.

SOWING: In late spring, start off under glass. Soak the seeds overnight, then sow them 2.5cm (1in) deep on their sides in individual pots. Harden off when all danger of frost has passed and plant outside under a cold frame when two or three true leaves appear. Remove the frame when it warms up. Or station-sow seeds outside from early summer in pre-warmed soil. Sow two seeds at each station: push them into the hole, on their sides. Remove the weaker one when the first true leaves appear. Space bush varieties 90cm (3ft) each way; trailing, 1.8m (6ft) each way.

GROWING: Support trailing varieties with stakes, tying in as necessary. Feed fortnightly and keep well watered – cucurbits are thirsty plants.

PESTS AND DISEASES: Powdery mildew, cucumber mosaic virus, slugs and snails. Red spider mite and whitefly, especially under glass.

COMPANION PLANTING: Dill repels red spider mite.

HARVESTING: Ready in 8–10 weeks. Pick young courgettes when 10–13cm (4–5in) long, or 6cm (2½in) in diameter. Use a sharp knife to cut them away and pick daily to encourage further crops. Don't leave marrows too long or they will become tough, pick when 25cm (10in) long – if your thumbnail goes in easily they are ready. Remove before first frosts and store in a cool, frost-free place.

CUCUMBERS (*Cucumis sativus*)

There are two types of cucumber: the greenhouse one is longer and smoother-skinned than the ridged outdoor one, but hybrid and Japanese varieties are smoother and rounder. Choose a bush or trailing variety. Gherkins are small cucumbers.

SOWING:
In the greenhouse: in early spring, sow seeds individually into small pots of moist compost, pot on to 30cm (12in) pots when plants are 15cm (6in) high.

Outside: in late spring, start off under glass in biodegradable pots. Sow two seeds per pot and thin to the strongest one. Harden off once they have three true leaves. A few weeks before planting out, dig out a hole 30cm (12in) deep and wide, and half-fill with well-rotted manure, then return the soil to form a mound at the top. Leave 75cm (30in) between each hole. Plant a little less deeply than they were in the pot to avoid fungal infection.

GROWING:
In the greenhouse: provide supports for tall varieties and pinch out once they reach the top of the string or cane; pinch out growing tips of bush varieties. Water regularly around plants not over them, and mist to keep air moist. Feed fortnightly, starting six weeks after transplanting.

Outside: Protect with cloches if weather turns cold. Keep well watered – around, not over the plant – and mulched. Provide support for trailing varieties and nip out the growing tip when plant reaches the top of the support. Once fruits start to swell, feed weekly with a liquid fertiliser.

PESTS AND DISEASES:
In the greenhouse: powdery mildew, red spider mite, whitefly.

Outside: powdery mildew, cucumber mosaic virus, slugs, aphids.

COMPANION PLANTING: Dill repels red spider mite.

HARVESTING Ready in 12–14 weeks. Cut off with a sharp knife when large enough – about 15–20cm (6–8in) – which will encourage further fruiting. Clear the ground after the first frosts.

SUMMER SQUASHES (*Cucurbita* species and hybrids)

In a variety of spectacular ornamental shapes, summer squashes can be bush, trailing or semi-trailing varieties.

SOWING: In early spring, sow seeds on their sides, 1cm (½in) deep in individual 8cm (3in) pots. Harden off and plant out after the last frosts to the same depth as they were in the pots. A few weeks before planting out, prepare individual planting holes: dig out a hole 45cm (18in) wide and deep. Mix the soil with the same amount of compost or rotted manure and put back in the hole, leaving a mound on the surface. Leave 90cm (3ft) between bush varieties; 1.8m (6ft) for trailing. Mulch the surface, then water in the young plant.

GROWING: Protect with cloches if weather turns cold. Pinch out growing tips on trailing types when 30–38cm (12–15in) high and provide support. Keep mulched and water weekly in dry weather. Feed with a nitrogen-rich fertiliser once fruits start to form.

PESTS AND DISEASES: Powdery mildew, cucumber mosaic virus, slugs, snails.

COMPANION PLANTING: Sunflowers will offer some shade.

HARVESTING: Ready in 8 weeks. Cut off using a sharp knife. To store, leave to dry in the sun (or under glass) for up to two weeks, then store nestled in straw in a dry frost-free place.

PUMPKINS AND WINTER SQUASHES
(Cucurbita maxima)

Like their summer cousins, pumpkins and winter squashes come in a variety of ornamental shapes and sizes. There are bush varieties, but they are mostly trailing plants.

SOWING: Sow under cover in individual pots in late spring and continue as for summer squashes.

GROWING: Plant out once last frosts have finished, but protect with fleece or cloches if the weather turns cold. Once established, water only when very hot and dry. Mulch well and feed with a liquid fertiliser every few weeks. Protect fruits by laying on a board or a bed of straw. Remove growing tip once three fruits have set.

PESTS AND DISEASES: Rabbits, deer, slugs, snails, powdery mildew, aphids.

COMPANION PLANTING: Marigolds (tagetes), nasturtiums or any 'sacrifice' plant to attract the aphids away from the crop.

HARVESTING: Ready in 12–20 weeks. Once they sound hollow when tapped, cut off leaving some of the stalk. Leave in the sun or under glass for several days to dry out completely. Store in a dry, frost-free place.

SALADS AND LEAVES

Salad leaves are the ideal intercrop as they are low and fast growing and are tolerant of most soil conditions, but still rotate them year on year as a precaution against soil disease. Sow seeds every few weeks during the season for a continuous supply. Take care when transplanting as they don't like their roots being disturbed. Always tear, never cut, the leaves away from the plant.

SWISS CHARD (*Beta vulgaris* subsp. *cicla* var. *flavescens*)

Cultivated for both its foliage and bright red, yellow, pink, white and orange stems and midribs, Swiss chard is easy to grow as long as it has a fertile, moist soil. Often, a spring sowing will last well into winter.

SOWING: Pre soak seeds the night before and start off in seed trays under cover in spring for summer and autumn harvesting. Transplant outside to 25cm (9in) apart with 45cm (18in) between rows. Sow again in late summer for winter crops.

GROWING: Keep weed-free and well watered during dry

weather. Feed with a high-nitrogen fertiliser as needed. Protect winter crops with cloches or a cold frame.

PESTS AND DISEASES: Generally trouble free.

HARVESTING: Cut off large leaves as you need them, but not too close to the stem. To harvest the whole plant, leave 5cm (2in) of the stem above the ground to resprout.

CHICORY (*Cichorium intybus*)

There are two types of chicory: heading, which includes the sugarloaf chicory and radiccio; and forcing, which refers to Witloof or Belgian chicory, which produces 'chicons'. They don't like too rich a soil, but don't mind a little shade.

SOWING: Start off heading types in modules in early spring or broadcast seeds in situ when the weather warms up and thin to 30cm (12in) apart. Sow forcing varieties in rows 30cm (12in) apart in late spring and thin to 20cm (8in).

GROWING: Keep weed free and water when dry. Blanch heading varieties by tying the leaves together and leaving for 10 days. For forcing varieties, cut off the head in autumn and cover the roots with a 15cm (6in) ridge of soil, then top with a cloche, straw or leafmould. To force indoors, dig up in late autumn, trim the leaves to 2.5cm (1in) from the roots and store in boxes of moist compost, covered with more compost.

PESTS AND DISEASES: Slugs, snails, caterpillars.

HARVESTING: Heading varieties ready in 8–12 weeks; forcing, 26 weeks, plus forcing time. Heading varieties: pick young leaves as needed or the head once it has turned white. Forcing varieties: if left outside, they will be ready the following spring; indoors, they'll be ready four to six weeks after covering when they are 8–10cm (3–4in) long.

ENDIVE *(Cichorium endiva)*

Endive comes with frilly leaves (frisée) for summer and autumn eating, or as a broad-leaved plant (batavian or escarole), which will survive a light frost and with protection grow on into winter.

SOWING: Sow frisée in situ from early summer and broad-leaved from late summer. Sow thinly 1cm (½in) deep and thin to 30–40cm (12–16in) apart.

GROWING: Keep weed-free, water in dry conditions and mulch. Cover broad-leaved varieties with a cloche when weather turns frosty. Blanch to remove the bitterness: loosely tie the leaves together, then cover with a bucket one or two weeks before harvesting. If you just want to blanch the centre, cover it with an old plate.

PESTS AND DISEASES: Slugs, aphids, caterpillars.

HARVESTING: Ready in 12–16 weeks. Pick individual leaves or cut off the head and leave the roots for the plant to resprout.

LETTUCE *(Lactuca sativa)*

The many different varieties of lettuce mean it is available all year, some in mixed seed packets or as cut-and-come-again types – whatever you choose, look for those labelled bolt- and disease-resistant. They all need a light, fertile, moisture-retentive soil.

SOWING: Early and late varieties are sown under cover, summer and spring in situ. Sow in modules for transplanting, or in 1cm (½in) deep drills and thin out when about 5cm (2in) high to 15–30cm (6–12in), depending on the variety.

Transplant when they have six true leaves, making sure the leaves are just above the ground to prevent rotting. Sow spring varieties under cloches in late autumn and thin out in spring.

GROWING: Keep weed-free, water when dry and mulch.

PESTS AND DISEASES: Birds, slugs, snails, aphids, chafer grubs, cutworm.

COMPANION PLANTING: Any 'sacrifice' plant to attract aphids away from the crop.

HARVESTING: Ready in 8–12 weeks. Pick leaves as needed; cut heads when they look well formed; start picking cut-and-come-again crops when they're about 10cm (4in) high. All varieties may sprout again if you cut away at the base and leave the root in the ground.

SPINACH (*Spinacia oleracea*)

Spinach needs a rich, moisture-retentive soil, neutral to alkaline, to do well. There are varieties for both summer and winter.

SOWING: Pre-soak seeds overnight and sow in situ, 2cm (¾in) deep, in rows 30cm (12in) apart. Thin alternate plants to 15cm (8in) apart. Sow summer varieties in early spring, winter ones in late summer and early autumn. For cut-and-come-again crops, sow thinly every few weeks from spring to summer, spaced 10cm (4in) apart.

GROWING: Keep weed-free and well-watered to prevent bolting. Feed with a high-nitrogen liquid fertiliser as needed. Net if birds are a problem and cover to protect winter varieties from frosts.

PESTS AND DISEASES: Bolting, downy mildew, slugs, snails, birds.

HARVESTING: Ready in 10–12 weeks. Pick leaves before they toughen from several different plants rather than just the one.

AMERICAN LAND CRESS (*Barbarea vulgaris*)

A peppery cress that tastes a little like watercress. Grow in a fertile soil in moist shade.

SOWING: Sow from spring through to late summer in drills, 1cm (½in) deep with rows 30cm (12in) apart. Thin to 15cm (6in).

GROWING: Keep weed-free and well watered in dry conditions. Do not allow to dry out or the leaves will coarsen.

PESTS AND DISEASES: Flea beetle.

HARVESTING: Ready in 12 weeks. Pick leaves as needed. Successive sowing should provide crops into winter. Save seed for sowing the following season.

ROCKET (*Eruca vesicaria* subsp. *sativa*)

Easy to grow in almost any soil. Site somewhere that is shaded at the height of the summer.

SOWING: Sow from late spring to early autumn at four-weekly intervals in situ. Sow in drills, 15cm (6in) apart, and thin to 15cm (6in). Sow in a cold frame in late autumn for winter crops.

GROWING: Keep weed-free and well watered in dry conditions.

PESTS AND DISEASES: Usually trouble free.

HARVESTING: Ready in 6–8 weeks. Pick leaves as needed or cut whole plants while still small, leaving stumps to resprout. Self-seeds well.

LAMB'S LETTUCE/CORN SALAD (*Valerianella locusta*)

A small, hardy annual that will provide crops for most of the year. Adaptable to all soil conditions.

SOWING: Sow every few weeks from spring to late summer. Sow in drills, 1cm (½in) deep with 30cm (12in) between rows. Thin to 20cm (8in) when they have three true leaves.

GROWING: Keep weed-free and well watered in dry conditions. Provide cover for winter crops.

PESTS AND DISEASES: May be affected by slugs and snails.

HARVESTING: Ready in 8 weeks. Pick odd leaves as required. Collect seeds for sowing the following season.

STEM VEGETABLES

Grown for their edible stems, all varieties will bolt if conditions are not right. They need a very rich, moisture-retentive soil, so dig in plenty of organic matter in autumn.

CELERY (*Apium graveolens* var. *dulce*)

There are two types of celery: self-blanching or summer celery, and trench or winter celery. Growing from seed poses lots of problems; it's less trouble to buy in young plants.

SOWING:
Self-blanching: In early summer, arrange the plants in a square block, 20cm (8in) apart so they give each other shade, and cover with fleece or cloches to protect from slugs.

Trench celery: Prepare the ground the previous autumn. Dig a trench 30cm (12in) deep and wide and half-fill it with well-rotted compost or manure. Fill in with soil to about 5cm (2in) below ground level. Plant the young plants in a row 30–45cm (12–18in) apart.

GROWING: Keep weed-free, well watered and give a weekly liquid feed. Mulch and check regularly for slugs.
Self-blanching: Remove cover after four weeks.

Trench celery: When the plants are 30cm (12in) high, tie the tops loosely together and start earthing-up – add 8cm (3in) of soil every three weeks as they grow, always leaving a third of the plant above ground. Alternatively, fit a loose collar of cardboard or newspaper, or slip over a piece of plastic pipe.

PESTS AND DISEASES: Celery fly, celery leaf spot, cutworm, slugs and snails.

HARVESTING:
Self-blanching: Ready in 26 weeks. Cut individual stems or lift the whole plant when stems are crisp and before leaves become pithy. Clear before the first frosts and store in a cool shed.

Trench celery: Ready in 40 weeks. Clear away soil and lift carefully. To store, wash and remove excess leaves and pack upright in boxes with damp sand around the roots. Keep in a cool, frost-free place.

CELERIAC *(Apium graveolens* var. *rapaceum)*

Hardier and less temperamental than celery, so easier to grow. Will do well in a damp patch.

SOWING: Start off seeds under cover in mid to late spring. Harden off, then plant outside after the last frosts. Plant so the crown is just above soil level, 30cm (12in) apart, with 45cm

(18in) between rows. Protect against slugs.

GROWING: Keep weed-free and well watered. Mulch and give a liquid seaweed feed every few weeks. Remove lower leaves and any side shoots in midsummer. In autumn, cover swollen bases with soil and protect during cold spells with a covering of straw.

PESTS AND DISEASES: Apart from slugs, usually trouble free, but can be subject to celery fly and celery leaf spot.

HARVESTING: Ready in 30 weeks. Lift as needed from mid autumn to early spring. Or clear the ground in late autumn and pack in damp sand and store in a cool place.

SOMETHING DIFFERENT

FLORENCE FENNEL (*Foeniculum vulgare* var. *azoricum*)

A fussy plant, with a tendency to bolt, but worth the effort. Avoid soil that is heavy, stony or poorly drained.

SOWING: Sow in situ when the soil has warmed up. Space seeds 30cm (12in) apart in a shallow drill with 30cm (12in) between rows. Sow again in late summer for an autumn crop.

GROWING: Keep weed-free and well watered. Mulch and check regularly for slugs. Earth up half-way around bulbs as they start to swell or tie a cardboard collar around them. Protect late sowings with a covering of fleece.

PESTS AND DISEASES: Slugs.

HARVESTING: Ready in 10–12 weeks. Lift carefully using a fork, or cut the bulb off just above ground level and leave the stump to throw out feathery leaves, which can be used for flavouring. Store bulbs in a cool, dry place.

PERENNIALS

This is a group of vegetables that can be left in one spot for up to five years or more. Before planting, clear and prepare the ground well and dig in plenty of organic matter, then feed or mulch annually. Move the crops to new ground when they need replacing.

ASPARAGUS *(Asparagus officinalis)*

Although you have to wait for up to three years, once asparagus starts cropping it will continue to do so for 20 years or more. Prepare the bed the autumn before sowing. Dig a trench 20cm (8in) deep and 1.2m (4ft) wide. Add manure or leafmould, and grit if the soil is heavy, then top up with about 7.5cm (3in) soil.

SOWING: In late spring, buy one-year-old crowns and plant 13cm (5in) deep in the trench, 45cm (18in) apart each way in two staggered rows. Fill in the trench.

GROWING: Hand weed regularly and keep well watered. In the autumn, cut the leaves down to the ground and mulch with well-rotted manure or compost. Protect from frosts and feed with a seaweed fertiliser the following spring.

PESTS AND DISEASES: Slugs, snails, asparagus beetle.

HARVESTING: Ready in 2–3 years. In the second year, around mid spring, cut off one or two spears from each plant when they're 20cm (8in) tall. Cut them with a sharp knife 5cm (2in) below the surface. Continue for six weeks. In the third year, you can harvest for up to eight weeks.

CARDOON *(Cynara cardunculus)*

Once its blanched stems were a popular vegetable, but now the cardoon is more often grown as a border plant for its dramatic foliage and thistle-like flowers. It grows to 1.8m (6ft).

SOWING: In late spring, sow three seeds per module under glass, thin to the strongest and plant out once all danger of frosts has passed. Or, station-sow in situ in early summer: sow three seeds 5cm (2in) deep in each station, leaving 60cm (24in) between stations. Thin out to the strongest.

GROWING: Keep weed-free and well watered in dry conditions. Feed weekly with a liquid fertiliser. Stake when they're about 30cm (12in) high. Blanch in late summer or early autumn: pull the stems loosely together and tie collars of newspaper or brown paper around the stems. Earth up the base and leave for four weeks.

PESTS AND DISEASES: Aphids.

COMPANION PLANTING: Any 'sacrifice' plant to attract aphids away from the crop.

HARVESTING: Ready in six months. Dig up the plant and cut away the leaves and roots. Divide the roots, snip off the offsets and plant up for next year.

GLOBE ARTICHOKE (*Cynara scolymus*)

Globe artichokes do not like cold, wet soil. Position them in sunshine and protect from winds. They grow to 1.5m (5ft) so make a good screening crop. As they're not always reliable grown from seed, buy small plants from a reputable nursery in the first instance, then propagate rooted suckers that appear in spring. Globe artichokes crop best in their second and third year.

SOWING: Plant in situ early to mid spring 90cm (3ft) apart each way, with the crown just below the surface of the soil.

GROWING: Keep weed-free and well watered. Mulch to retain moisture. Feed with liquid seaweed every few weeks during the summer. Earth up the base in autumn and cover the crown with straw in winter.

PESTS AND DISEASES: Aphids and slugs.

COMPANION PLANTING: Any 'sacrifice' plant to attract aphids or slugs away from the crop.

HARVESTING: Ready in 18 months. Cut the main head while it's still tight, still retaining part of the stem. Cut the side shoots later on. In subsequent years, the plant will produce more side shoots, remove the side buds if you want larger heads.

RHUBARB (*Rheum x hybridum*)

Not a fussy plant, but doesn't like shade. The juicy stems are usually ready for eating from late spring through to summer, but a crop can be forced in late winter ready for early spring. The leaves are poisonous.

SOWING: In late autumn, plant crowns 90cm (3ft) apart each way so the buds are just above the soil.

GROWING: Keep weed-free and water well in dry conditions, avoiding the crown. Mulch well to retain moisture. Apply a top dressing of well-rotted manure in spring and a nitrogen feed if needed. Cut off the flowering seedheads.

PESTS AND DISEASES: Slugs, snails, honey fungus.

HARVESTING: Ready in 2 years from late spring. Pull down the stem at the base, twist and pull off. Leave at least three stems behind on each plant. Continue harvesting until midsummer. Divide plants every three to four years. To force rhubarb: anytime from midwinter onwards, cover dormant crowns with an upturned bucket or a purpose-made clay pot. Stems will be ready within three to five weeks.

FRUITING VEGETABLES

Fruiting vegetables are hungry, thirsty crops. They will need a sunny, sheltered spot, a fertile soil that has had plenty of organic material dug in and regular feeding. Start them off under glass and, up to a week before planting out, cover the soil with cloches or polythene to warm it up.

SWEET PEPPERS (*Capsicum annuum/Grossum group*)

Peppers prefer slightly higher temperatures than other fruiting vegetables, so grow in a sheltered raised bed or against a sunny wall if possible. Most varieties start off green, then turn to red, yellow or purple as they ripen.

SOWING: Sow inside in mid spring in seed trays, then pot on to 11cm (4in) pots when there are three true leaves. Harden off and plant outside 45cm (18in) apart each way once all danger of frosts has passed and the first flowers are forming.

GROWING: Keep weed-free and well watered. Mulch to retain moisture. Stake plants and feed regularly with a general fertiliser once flowers form, then change to a high-potash fertiliser.

PESTS AND DISEASES: Aphids.

COMPANION PLANTING: Any 'sacrifice' plant to attract aphids away from the crop.

HARVESTING: Ready in 12 weeks. Gather while green to encourage more fruit to form, or leave on the plant to change colour. Dig up any remaining plants still bearing fruit before the first frosts and hang in a frost-free shed or a greenhouse.

CHILLIES *(Capsicum annuum/Longum group)*

There are many different varieties of chilli, which vary from mild to the pungent *Capsicum frutescens* (bird's-eye chilli).

SOWING: Sow hot chilli varieties as for sweet peppers in late winter; the milder varieties up to early spring. Grow on and transplant as for sweet peppers.

GROWING: Treat as sweet peppers, but pinch out the growing tips when plants are 20cm (8in) tall to encourage side shoots.

PESTS AND DISEASES: Aphids.

Removing side shoots from tomatoes

COMPANION PLANTING: Any 'sacrifice' plant to attract aphids away from the crop.

HARVESTING: Ready in 18–20 weeks. Gather when fully ripe. Dig up any remaining plants still bearing fruit before the first frosts and hang in a frost-free shed or a greenhouse.

TOMATO (*Lycopersicon esculentum*)

From the same family as the potato – so never grow the two together as they can pass potato blight between each other. There are cordon, bush and dwarf varieties, in sizes ranging from the small cherry tomato up to the large beef tomato. When growing outside, make sure you choose an outdoor type and not an indoor one, intended for growing in a greenhouse.

SOWING: About eight weeks before the last frosts, sow seeds 2cm (¾in) deep in seed trays in a greenhouse. When there are three true leaves, pot on into 11cm (4in) pots. Once all danger of frosts has passed, harden off before planting out. Space bush varieties 60cm (24in) apart and cordons 45cm (18in).

GROWING: Keep weed-free and water regularly – do not allow to dry out, especially once fruits start to form, as this will cause them to split. Apply a tomato fertiliser every week. Remove yellowing lower leaves as they appear.
Cordons: Tie the main stem to a strong support and pinch out the side shoots as they appear. Nip off the top growing tip in late summer.

Sowing sweetcorn in squares

Bush: Mulch with straw to keep the fruits clean.

PESTS AND DISEASES: Blossom end rot, potato blight.

HARVESTING: Ready in 16-20 weeks. Gather fruits as they ripen. Before the first frosts, clear all unripe fruits and bring inside to ripen on a sunny windowsill, or hang in trusses, or put in a paper bag or drawer with a ripe banana.

SWEETCORN (*Zea mays*)

Sweetcorn comes in a variety of colours. There are early, mid-season and late varieties so you can have fresh corn over a longer period. The sugars in sweetcorn turn to starch very quickly after picking, so it doesn't store well.

SOWING: As the roots don't like disturbance, sow individual seeds in modules or small pots, giving the root ball a chance to form. Sow in a greenhouse about six weeks before the last frosts, then harden off before planting outside when the seedlings are about 7.5cm (3in) high. Grow in blocks to aid pollination: plant the seedlings in groups of four, 30–45cm (12–18in) apart both ways.

GROWING: Weed by hand and mulch well once established. Water if dry, when the flowers appear and when the cobs start to swell. Earth up as plants grow to give extra support. Stake if necessary.

PESTS AND DISEASES: Mice, birds.

HARVESTING: Ready in 7-18 weeks. Test for ripeness when the tassels turn brown: push a fingernail into the kernel, if the juice is milky, it's ready. Support the stem with one hand and twist off the cob with the other.

Aubergine (Solanum melongena)

Fruits can be long or round, white, yellow or black as well as purple. They need a warm, very sunny spot to thrive.

SOWING: Sow in late winter or early spring in a greenhouse. Sow seeds in modules or a seed tray and prick out when 5cm (2in) high into 11cm (4in) pots. Harden off and plant outside 45cm (18in) apart each way, when all danger of frosts has passed and the first flowers have appeared.

GROWING: Keep weed-free and well watered. Mulch and stake. Feed regularly with a general fertiliser, changing to a tomato fertiliser once fruits appear. Pinch off growing tips when plants are 30cm (12in) high to encourage more side shoots.

PESTS AND DISEASES: Aphids may be a problem.

COMPANION PLANTING: Any 'sacrifice' plant to attract aphids away from the crop.

HARVESTING: Ready in 18-20 weeks. Pick the fruits when fully coloured and still shiny (they become bitter as the skin becomes dull). Protect still fruiting plants with fleece on autumn nights, or lift the whole plant and hang in a cool place.

Okra/Lady's Fingers/Bhindi (Hibiscus esculentus)

The plants grow to 1.2m (4ft) high and produce pretty yellow flowers. You may need to protect them with cloches or fleece if the temperature drops.

SOWING: In mid to late spring, pre-soak the seeds the day before sowing in a heated propagator set to 16°C (61°F). Transplant to individual 9cm (3½in) pots when big enough to handle. Harden off when about 30cm (12in) tall, then transplant outside in early summer, 60cm (24in) apart both ways. Two weeks before moving outside, warm up the ground first with black polythene or cloches.

GROWING: Keep weed-free and well watered. Mulch to keep warm and retain moisture. Stake and feed weekly. Pinch out growing tips periodically to encourage sideshoots.

PESTS AND DISEASES: Aphids may be a problem.

COMPANION PLANTING: Any 'sacrifice' plant.

HARVESTING: Ready in 18-20 weeks. Pick pods regularly when they are 7.5cm (3in) long, bright green and firm to the touch, cutting them off the stem with a sharp knife. Handle carefully as they bruise easily. Okra doesn't store well.

COMMON PROBLEMS

Pests and diseases are inevitable, but they can be dealt with. In the first instance, make it more difficult for them to get a hold by looking after your plot, the soil and your plants. Don't leave piles of debris and weeds around where predators can hide and diseases breed. Keep the soil healthy with regular weeding, digging and mulching, adding plenty of organic material so it's humus rich and water-retentive. Buy disease-resistant seed varieties when available, choosing organic seeds and young plants where possible. Don't skip any of the stages of cultivation, which can result in weak, vulnerable plants.

ENCOURAGE FRIENDLY PREDATORS with companion planting and by providing suitable habitats for them: black beetles and newts feed on soil pests; ladybirds, lacewings and hoverflies devour aphids, mealy bugs and small caterpillars; toads, frogs and hedgehogs eat slugs (as do birds, of course, but they can be a mixed blessing!).

Practise crop rotation to help prevent problems arising and avoid chemical pesticides unless there is no other course open to you. Garden Organic (formerly known as The Henry Doubleday Research Association) has a list of recommended organic chemicals but they should only be used as a last resort. In most cases, they are active for no longer than a day but they may be harmful to beneficial insects too and toxic to fish, so need to be applied with care.

PESTS

APHIDS: They suck the sap of plants and secrete honeydew, which creates a sooty mould. They carry viruses and diseases. Rub off with your fingers or blast with a spray of water or a weak solution of washing-up liquid or soap. Encourage natural predators – ladybirds, hoverflies, lacewings. Start off vulnerable varieties early under cover and protect with fleece when you can.

ASPARAGUS BEETLE: The adults are 6mm (¼in) long, black and yellow with a red thorax; the larvae are dark grey and 10mm (½in) long. The adults emerge in late spring after laying their eggs. If left, both larvae and adults will eat the spears and foliage. Check regularly, pick them off by hand and burn the foliage at the end of the season.

BIRDS: Cover vulnerable seedlings and young plants with chicken wire, netting or fleece. Hang bird scarers: old CDs, strips of aluminium foil – or anything that swirls and catches the light – are effective.

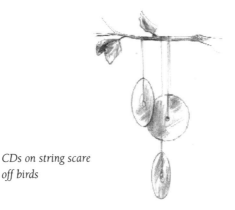

CDs on string scare off birds

BLACKFLY: See aphids.

BLACK BEAN APHID: See aphids.

BOLTING: Under pressure, the plant panics and flowers before it's ready. Give it the right conditions and choose bolt-resistant varieties.

CABBAGE WHITE BUTTERFLIES: The caterpillar is hairy and yellow with black markings and will eat the leaves of brassicas. Check regularly for infestation: pick off affected leaves; wash off with water or a salt water spray; or protect the crop with fine mesh. Or try the biological control, *Bacillus thuringiensis*.

CABBAGE ROOT FLY: The adults are grey and about 1cm (½in) long and lay their eggs on or near the plant, where they overwinter in the soil. The white maggot burrows into the roots and does the damage. Wilting and poor growth are among the first signs of infestation. Cover the soil with fleece or fine mesh after sowing or planting out; or provide individual plants with 10cm (4in) collars of carpet or cardboard.

Collars around cabbages keep off pests

CARROT FLY: Adult flies are about 1.5cm (¾in) long, black with a reddish head and orange wings; the larvae are slightly longer and creamy-white. The larvae tunnel into the roots to feed. Cover the crop with fleece or fine mesh, or erect a barrier 60cm (24in) high – the females will not fly above that height. The fly is attracted by scent, so space seedlings wide apart to avoid the necessity of thinning, but if you do need to, pull them up carefully on a dry evening with no wind (harvest in the same conditions). Choose disease-resistant varieties and plant alongside onions or marigolds, as their smell confuses the fly.

CATERPILLARS: The larvae of moths, butterflies, etc., feed on leaves, stems or roots. Pick them off when seen or spray with a salt water mix. Or try the biological control, *Bacillus thuringiensis*.

CELERY FLY: The tiny adult flies lay eggs on the foliage and the small maggots burrow into and through the leaves, causing white or brownish blisters to appear as they go. Remove the maggots as they appear; pull off and burn affected leaves.

CUTWORMS: The larvae of noctuid moths, cutworms are 'c'-shaped caterpillars, up to 2.5cm (1in) long, usually brown, yellow or green. They feed at night, eating their way along a row of vegetables, severing the whole crop. Keep the area weed free as that's where the moths lay their eggs. The caterpillars will be visible at night in torchlight – pick them off and destroy them and protect vulnerable plants with cardboard collars. Be especially vigilant in dry summers.

CHAFER GRUBS: The adults are about 1cm (½in) long with either a metallic green or black head. The larvae have white bodies curved into a 'c' shape with three pairs of legs near the head. Pick off and destroy. If the soil is badly infested, water a pathogenic nematode, *Heterorhabditis megidis*, into the soil in the late summer or early autumn.

DEER: Quite hard to keep out without erecting a 3m (10ft) high wire fence. Although a smaller, double set of fences, set 90cm–1.2m (3–4ft) apart, may work, as deer don't like to get trapped between them. Shiny objects such as old CDs may deter them, as will loud noises and human hair.

EARWIGS: They hide in sheltered places during the day and come out at night to feed on foliage. They are visible by torchlight and can be picked off, or collected each morning in upturned flower pots filled with straw and suspended on canes set among affected plants. Earwigs do also feed on other small pests and their eggs, so their presence is a mixed blessing.

FLEA BEETLE: The adults emerge in spring. They are small, black or metallic blue and shiny, and can be seen jumping off leaves when disturbed. They leave small holes on the leaf, which turn brown. They can destroy seedlings and hinder the growth of older plants. The larvae feed on the roots, but most plants survive this. Protect crops in the vulnerable stages by growing under cloches or fleece. If plants are infested, smear grease on a board, put under the plant and give it a good shake, then dispose of board and flea beetles.

MEALY APHIDS: See aphids.

MICE: Protect plants with cloches. Set traps under propped-up roof tiles or pieces of slate.

MOLES: They dislike the smell of caper spurge (*Euphorbia lathyris*). Mole traps are available from garden centres.

ONION EELWORM: Microscopic worms in the soil that cause swelling and distortion of onion plants. There is no cure. If you're unlucky enough to get it, clear the plot and don't grow onions there for three or four years.

ONION FLY: The adults emerge in late spring and lay their eggs on and around the plant. The small white maggots tunnel into the roots, causing the plant to rot. Cover plants with fine net or fleece early in the season. The flies find the plant using their sense of smell, so be careful when thinning the seedlings or grow sets instead. Plant alongside carrots to confuse them, or try a strong-smelling flower crop such as marigolds. Lift any affected plants and destroy.

PEA MOTH: The adults lay their eggs on the flowers and the resulting tiny caterpillars develop inside the pods and eat the peas. The risk is highest in mid-season, so plant early or late to avoid the breeding season. Protect mid-season crops with fine mesh or fleece when in flower.

Netting over beds

POTATO CYST EELWORM: The eggs can stay in the ground for many years. The larvae feed on the roots and the first signs are dying leaves starting from the bottom of the plant and working upwards. If you get it, the only thing you can do is clear the ground and not plant potatoes or tomatoes there again for at least seven years. Plant a crop of *Sinapis alba*, a mustard green manure, to help clear the soil of eelworms.

RABBITS: Erect wire netting around plants, but it will need to be buried at least 45cm (18in) deep and be 90cm (3ft) high. Rabbits hate rhubarb plants, so plant offshoots near vulnerable plants or create a barrier with the leaves.

RED SPIDER MITE: Usually found in the greenhouse, they are now appearing more often in the garden, especially in a long, hot summer. They are tiny mites that start off as brown or yellow, changing to orange-red in the autumn. A pale mottling appears on the leaves, or a fine, silky web, and sometimes you can see the mites clustered on the underside. Spray with a good dose of water, or introduce a predatory mite, *Phytoseiulus persimilis*, into the greenhouse.

SLUGS AND SNAILS: They like warm, moist weather and come out at night. Collect and destroy them (drop them into a salt water solution if you can bear it), checking under leaves or other debris. Leave propped-up pieces of terracotta or slate tile near plants where the slugs and snails will collect – especially if you leave some rotting vegetation underneath. Sink plastic pots of beer into the soil and empty out regularly. Protect plants with cloches or surround them with sharp gravel, egg shells, soot or ash. Place a serrated collar of plastic or a copper band around young plants. Encourage natural predators such as hedgehogs, frogs, toads and birds.

WHITEFLY: Another greenhouse inhabitant that is making its way outdoors. The tiny flying insects suck the sap on the underside of leaves and secrete a sticky honeydew. Plant a 'sacrifice' plant such as marigolds (*tagetes*) or basil to attract the whitefly, or spray with a weak dilution of soap. Try the biological control, *Encarsia formosa*, a tiny parasitic wasp.

WIREWORMS: The larvae of orange click beetles and leatherjackets that live in the ground and eat their way through roots and stems. They are about 2.5cm (1in) long with orange bodies. They are mostly found in grassland, so keep the ground weed-free and dig over in winter when they will come to the top and provide a meal for the birds.

DISEASES

BLOSSOM END ROT: A tough leathery patch that appears at the base of the tomato, caused by dryness at the roots or too acid a soil. Pick off the fruits and compost them. Water the plants well and regularly.

CELERY LEAF SPOT: Caused by a fungus usually found in the seed. Tiny brown spots appear on the leaves and spread in damp conditions. Cut away infected parts of the plant and destroy them.

CHOCOLATE SPOT: A fungal disease that causes brown spots to appear on leaves and which spreads in wet weather. Pull out and destroy any leaves that are badly affected. Prevent by providing a rich, well-drained soil and good air circulation.

CLUBROOT: A fungal disease that affects brassicas and root vegetables and for which there is no cure. The roots become distorted, causing a series of tuberous swellings. If your plants are wilting for no obvious reason, dig them up and check the roots. If infected, burn the whole crop as soon as possible and disinfect boots and tools. Clubroot can live in the soil for 20 years. Avoidance or cleansing measures include adding lime to acid soil (clubroot loves acid soil) to bring it up to pH7 or above. Be rigorous about practising a strict crop rotation to prevent the disease building up. Keep weeds such as shepherd's purse and bitter cress under control as they are alternative hosts, as are mustard green manures. Grow disease-resistant fast-maturing varieties rather than long-term crops, such as Brussels sprouts. Raise seedlings in sterile compost and buy from a reliable source.

CUCUMBER MOSIAC VIRUS: The leaves develop yellow patterns and the fruit becomes distorted. Lift and burn affected plants. Buy disease-resistant varieties.

DOWNY MILDEW: The top of the leaves turn yellow with grey patches underneath. It thrives in damp, warm conditions. Remove infected leaves and burn them. Ensure there is good air circulation and clear away any weeds. Water at the base of plants in the morning rather than the evening.

HONEY FUNGUS: White streaks appear in the crown, orange toadstools may grow up around the plant. Dig out the affected plants and burn them.

LEEK RUST: Orange pustules appear on the leaves, often in damp conditions. Not harmful, but burn any affected leaves. Avoid overwatering.

MOULD: A green or yellowish fungal growth appears on the undersides of leaves during long, wet spells. Dig up and burn affected plants.

ONION WHITE ROT: A fluffy white fungus that covers the base of the bulbs and the roots, causing the leaves to turn yellow and wilt. Dig up and burn the crop and leave for eight years before planting any of the onion family in the same ground again.

ONION NECK ROT: A grey, fluffy fungal growth that appears around the neck of the bulb once the onions have been in store for a few months. The onions become soft and discoloured. Choose quality sets for planting and allow for good air circulation both while growing and in storage. Check bulbs are not damaged before storing.

PARSNIP CANKER: Brown, red or black patches appear on the shoulder of the roots nearest the soil. The fungal infection enters through a hole, probably left by a carrot fly. There is no cure, but growing them under fleece can protect them from the carrot fly in the first instance.

POTATO BLIGHT: Brown blotches appear on leaves and stems caused by a mass of fungal spores. The fungus travels down into the tubers, which become soft, turn black and give off a bad smell. Remove and burn affected plants. Buy good quality, disease-resistant varieties. Space plants so there is plenty of air circulation and water around the base of the plant. Mulch to prevent spores reaching the tubers and clear the ground at the end of the season to prevent the disease lurking in the soil.

POWDERY MILDEW: Shows as a whitish dusty deposit on the leaves that can cause yellowing, distortion and leaf drop. It mainly affects young plants in dry soil when conditions are humid. Remove affected leaves and destroy badly affected plants. Keep plants well watered, applied from the bottom of the plant not from the top. Avoid overfeeding with nitrogen, which can cause weak, sappy growth. Look for disease-resistant varieties. Sulphur dust can limit damage, but use carefully as it is harmful to beneficial insects.

RUST: Pustules appear on the leaves, often in damp conditions. Not harmful, but burn any affected leaves. Avoid overwatering.

USEFUL ORGANISATIONS

Garden Organic,
Ryton Organic Gardens, Coventry CV8 3LG
(024 7630 3517; www.gardenorganic.org.uk)
*Europe's largest organic organisation offering advice, events,
gardens to visit, a regular magazine and access to the Heritage
Seed Library. Formerly Henry Doubleday Research Organisation.*

National Institute of Agricultural Botany (NIAB)
Huntington Road, Cambridge CB3 OLE
(01223 342200; www.niab.com)
*An independent bio-science research company offering
information on developments in plant varieties and seeds. Useful
publications include NIAB Veg Finder, new and interesting
varieties to grow, compiled each year by NIAB staff.*

National Vegetable Society, 5 Whitelow Road, Heaton Moor,
Stockport SK4 4BY (0161 442 7190; www.nvsuk.org.uk)
Help, advice and information on growing and showing produce.

Royal Horticultural Society, 80 Vincent Square,
London SW1P 2PE (020 7834 4333; www.rhs.org.uk)
*Well known worldwide. Advice, information, lectures, shows,
magazine, publications and an easy-to-negotiate informative
website.*

Self Sufficient 'ish' (www.selfsufficientish.com)
*An interactive website offering advice, information, recipes and
a general sharing of stories, ideas and knowledge.*

Soil Association, Bristol House, 40-56 Victoria Street, Bristol
BS1 6BY (0117 314 5000; www.soilassociation.org.uk)
*At the heart of the campaign for growing and eating organic
food, the association offers advice and information.*

SEED AND PLANT SUPPLIERS

BEANS AND HERBS
01985 844442;
www.beansandherbs.co.uk
*Organic vegetable and herb seeds,
including unusual varieties.*

THE CHILLI SEED COMPANY
015395 58110;
www.chileseeds.co.uk
*Chilli pepper seeds and a selection
of organic tomatoes.*

CHILTERN SEEDS
01229 581137;
www.chilternseeds.co.uk
*Wide selection of different varieties,
many rare and unusual.*

DOBIES SEEDS
0870 112 3625;
www.dobies.co.uk
*A comprehensive selection of seeds
and young plants.*

MR FOTHERGILL'S SEEDS LTD
01638 751161;
www.fothergills.co.uk
*Includes many new varieties including
organic and heritage.*

**THE ORGANIC GARDENING
CATALOGUE**
0845 130 1304;
www.organiccatalog.com
*The mail order catalogue for the
Garden Organic.*

THE REAL SEED COMPANY
01239 821107;
www.realseeds.co.uk
*Many heirloom varieties and all
open-pollinated (non-hybrid).*

SEEDS OF ITALY
020 8417 5020;
www.seedsofitaly.com
Comprehensive selection of

*Mediterranean vegetables – with over
90% produced in Italy.*

SUTTONS SEEDS
0800 783 8704;
www.suttons.co.uk
*Reliable producer of seeds – including
mixed packets – and young plants.*

TAMAR ORGANICS
01579 371087;
www.tamarorganics.co.uk
*No GM or treated seed, though some
non-organic, but all young plants are
organic.*

THOMAS ETTY ESQ
020 8466 6785;
www.thomasetty.co.uk
*An interesting collection of heritage
and unusual vegetable seeds.*

THOMPSON & MORGAN LTD
01473 688821;
www.thompson-morgan.com
*Trustworthy choice of seeds and young
plants.*

UNWINS SEEDS
01945 588522;
www.unwins-seeds.co.uk
*Well-established company offering
seeds and young plants.*

WILD ABOUT VEG
0845 300 4257;
www.wildaboutveg.com
*The seed catalogue from Heritage
Gardening, which includes heritage
and modern varieties.*

W ROBINSON & SONS
01524 791210;
www.mammothonion.co.uk
*If your ambition is to grow the
largest onion or biggest pumpkin,
this is where to buy your seed.*

GLOSSARY

ANNUAL A plant that completes its life cycle within one season.

BIENNIAL A plant that completes its life cycle within two years: growing in the first year, then flowering and fruiting in the second.

BOLT When a plant flowers and produces seed too early.

CATCH CROPPING (intercropping/undercropping) Growing a quick maturing crop between or under slower-growing ones.

CLOCHE Glass or plastic sheets used to protect young plants from cold weather or to warm up the ground before planting.

COLD FRAME An unheated frame fitted with glass or plastic sheets in which young plants are placed to offer some protection while acclimatising to outdoor conditions; or to give them a head start.

CROP ROTATION The practice of growing vegetables from the same family in a different plot each season to prevent the build-up of pests and diseases and maintain the nutrients in the soil.

DAMPING OFF When stems of emerging seedlings collapse as a result of a fungus rotting the stems and roots.

DIVIDE UP Splitting up a plant, down through the roots, using a sharp knife or spade. The sections are then replanted to grow on as separate plants.

DRILL A narrow, straight furrow created with a hoe or rake in which seeds are sown.

EARTHING UP Drawing up soil around the roots of plants. Done to stop them becoming green and poisonous (as for potatoes); to blanch stems; to provide an anchor for tall plants against wind rock.

HARDEN OFF Slowly acclimatising young, tender or half-hardy plants to outdoor conditions before moving them outside permanently.

HEEL-IN Storing mature crops in a shallow trench – upright or at an angle – which is then filled in and firmed down.

INTERCROP See catchcropping.

MIDRIB The central vein running from the stalk to the tip of a leaf.

MULCH A thick covering of well-rotted manure or compost, straw, leafmould etc applied to the soil. It helps the soil retain moisture (applied after watering or heavy rain); protects roots of plants in cold weather; keeps down weeds; and improves soil structure.

OFFSET A young plant attached to the main plant, often on or near the roots, which can be removed and grown on.

PERENNIAL A plant that lives for several years.

PINCH OUT To remove the growing tips of a plant (usually with finger and thumb) to encourage the growth of sideshoots.

POT ON To remove a seedling from an outgrown tray or pot into a larger pot filled with fresh compost.

PRE SOAK To soak seed in previously boiled water for a specified time to soften the seedcoat prior to sowing.

PRICK OUT To transfer seedlings or young plants from where they have germinated to a larger container filled with fresh compost.

ROOT CUTTING Cutting taken from vigorous roots during winter to grow on as a separate plant.

'SACRIFICE' PLANT A flowering plant, herb or vegetable planted next to a crop to attract pests and diseases away from the crop.

STATION SOW Sowing two or three seeds in the same hole.

SUBSOIL The layer of soil below the topsoil, which is less fertile and has a poorer structure.

SUCCESSIONAL SOWING Sowing little and often at regular intervals to provide a continuous supply of a particular vegetable.

THINNING Removing seedlings or plants to create more room and more resources for those left behind.

TOPSOIL The uppermost fertile layer of the soil.

TRANSPLANT Moving a seedling or young plant from its initial place of germination to a larger pot or the bed where it will grow to maturity.

TRUE LEAVES The first set of leaves produced after the initial seedling leaves.

WILT The effect on a plant of pest activity, a fungal disease or lack of water, causing it to collapse.

WIND ROCK The loosening of a plant's root system when the plant is buffeted by strong winds.

INDEX